SECRET HISTORY OF
'THE INTERNATIONAL'
WORKING MEN'S ASSOCIATION

By

Onslow Yorke

London
Spradabach Publishing
2025

SPRADABACH PUBLISHING
BM Box Spradabach
London WC1N 3XX

Secret History of 'The Internationa' Working Men's Association

First published in 1872
First Spradabach edition published 2025
© Spradabach Publishing 2025

Interior design by Alex Kurtagic

ISBN 978-1-909606-61-6

British Library Cataloguing-in-Publication Data:
A catalogue record for this book is available from the British Library.

Note

Her Majesty's Government has ordered some inquiries to he made in foreign countries as to the strength and purpose of the International Working Men's Association. Nimble pens are busy; and in time the public may receive a Blue Book, which some twenty persons will care to rend. Until this work is ready, these sketches may suggest how curious and important is the task on which our Secretaries of Legation are employed.

O. Y.

Geneva,
October 30th, 1871.

Table of Contents

List of Illustrations

Note on This Edition

The text on the present volume is based one the Strahan & Co. Publishers edition published in London 1872 and is reproduced here in its entirety.

The spelling, punctuation, and capitalisation appear as in the original. Italics have also been left as in the original, except in the titles of published works or songs, which have been taken out of quotation marks and italicised.

The original abbreviation 'M.' (Monsieur) has been spelled out where it begins a chapter and the M is a drop cap, to maintain typographical aesthetics.

All the photographs and illustrations are additions to the original for purposes of this edition.

A complement of editorial footnotes has been added and a complete index has been generated.

CHAPTER I

At St. Gervais

"Y ou propose to put down the system of hiring men to work, and paying them the wages of that work?" I ask a clever artisan, who has been good enough to explain to me the views and wishes of his class.

"We mean to put it down."

The scene is a small brasserie, in the suburb of St. Gervais, the industrial quarter of Geneva, where the workmen come to drink their beer. The men are sons of Grütli, members of the Democratic Alliance, followers of the International Association.[1] Do they ask for higher wages? No, they would abolish wages. They demand that hiring men at so much for the day shall cease. To take a salary is to be a slave. No man, they say, should have to seek for his employment. It should come to him, like morning light, as Heaven's best gift; and so it would, these sons of Grütli, members of the Democratic Alliance, and followers of the International pretend, if some few diabolical persons—chiefly kaisers, priests and bankers—were but swept away. "Our foes," says Jean Romande, his third bock at his lips, "are the financiers. They buy and sell us, soul and body, for their gain. They suck our blood, they eat our flesh, they kill us inch by inch and day by day. Financiers never work, like honest men; they lurk, all day, like tigers in a cave; and pounce upon their prey if it should come in sight. What palaces they build! And who can tell what mistresses they keep? But they have had their day. Let us combine our strength; we are the many and the masters; we have only to refuse their money, and to vote as one man for our class.

---

1   The Grütli Union (*Grütliverein*) was a Swiss workers' association founded in 1838. Initially focused on mutual aid and education for workers, it gradually evolved into a political force advocating for social reform and labour rights. By the 1860s, it leaned toward moderate socialism. The Democratic Alliance refers to the International Alliance of Socialist Democracy, a revolutionary anarchist organisation founded by Mikhail Bakunin in 1868. It promoted anti-authoritarian socialism and was critical of state-centred approaches like those advocated by Marx. The International Association is the International Working Men's Association, the subject of this work. —Ed.

Financing and oppression will go down, as priest-craft and imperialism have just gone down."

"But how do you propose to put down hire and wage?"

"By law. For we are men of peace; we raise our words against all acts of force; we only stand upon our rights; we make a study of the public good: and when we see our way to act, the thing will be already done."

"By popular vote, like any other change?"

"Why not? We are the many—the majority; our patrons and the bankers who abet them are the few. At an election they are nowhere. With their money they can buy up house and land; and in the bad old days, not wholly gone even now, they used to buy our votes; but we have come to see that what they buy is cheap to them and dear to us. A flask of beer, a civil speech, a grip of palms, and lo, our birthright gone! In former days our eyes were dim; we stuffed our ears with texts: we thought the last word had been said, when some one mumbled that a labourer is worthy of his hire. His hire! We have another gospel now. We say the labourer is worthy of his work"

"But is not that the same?"

"Excuse me—no! The factors and financiers say so; but they know the difference well. We mean that every man should have the fruit of what he plants and prunes; the whole fruit—not apart of it as now. We want the harvest for the husbandman, the chamois for the hunter, and the pine-log for the woodman."

3

"You would sweep away the owner and his agents?"

"We would have no owners of the soil. We have no owners of the air and of the waters. Every man can take his fill of air, and shoot his prey in the free vault of heaven. So every man can paddle on the lake,and drop his line for perch and pike. It is not so, I hear, in other lands your own for one?"

"The fact is so. We have, in truth, a number of reserved and private rights, descending to us from the feudal times; but we are also busy with the task of putting our abuses down."

"Your men of money—your financiers—will not suffer you to shoot and fish for your own pot and pan in God's own air and water. Good. Our men of money—our financiers—will not suffer us to rake and scythe the earth for our own pot and pan. Let them beware; the end is nigh"

"Then you have formed a plan?"

"A plan? Karl Marx has formed a plan. All things will be arranged in time; our duty is to organise, to study, to diffuse good principles, and to make our sections strong."

In naming Marx my guide is speaking of the International Working Men's Association—that mysterious body, which, according to its friends, is seeking, through pacific means and by the channel of existing laws, to soften manners, to adjust all quarrels, to remove monopolies and barriers, to protect the weak, to raise the humble, to console the poor, and make the meanest creature feel that he is still a brother and a man: but which, according to its enemies, is seeking through petroleum, powder, and the secret knife, to undo all the noblest work of time, to uproot property, to break through laws, to violate the family ties, to burn the altar and upset the throne. "We are the men of peace," says one side. "You have burnt down Paris" cries the other. "We are only a society of study," urge the first. "You are disturbing every country, from the Neva to the Hudson," shouts the second.

"You are rebels—you are outlaws; you have forfeited all human rights," exclaims the upper class.

"For what?" demands the working man; "for studying in your books, and in your schools, the laws which govern those great markets of the world, the labour market and the money market? Outlawed for trying to understand the law!"

"You study-fudge! You only care to rob, to ravage, and to burn. Behold your work—the charred and desolated city on the Seine! "Though it is only seven years old, the International Working Men's Association has passed through many stages. It can boast of youth, maturity, and age; for it has had in seven short years its pentecost, its schism, its transformation, its secession and its civil war.

A secret history is to be told; a sad and curious tale; the most instructive in the annals of our time.

International Exhibition, 1862

CHAPTER II

Two Paris Workmen

In the Summer days of 1862 the world was driving from all quarters into Cromwell Road to see the wonders of our second International Exhibition—crowds from east and west, from north and south, ambassadors from kings and kaisers, ministers from colonies, city corporations and republics, delegates from unions, mills and mines. While this great crowd was tearing into Cromwell Road to see what they should see—the riches of this world, and all the pomp and power of wealth—two workmen of the class which is the salt of Paris, Henri Tolain,[1] chaser in bronze, and Eugène Fribourg,[2] decorative en graver, had a waking dream. They thought there might be things to see in Cromwell Road beyond the pomp and pride of wealth; some inkling of the secret science which controls the rise and fall of wages, giving bread in plenty to the workman's children one day, and denying them a crust next day. Sitting at their benches in the Rue des Gravilliers, they had long been pondering on the labour question. They had heard of English strikes. They wished to learn how English artisans arrange the problems of apprenticeship and hours of work. In youth the two men had been politicians; they had dreamt of vast reforms; but time was wearing them away; a Bonaparte was on the throne; a golden age had not yet come; and now the social question seemed to them of deeper moment than the question of which regal house should reign in France. The rate of wages and the hours of work were things to them of life and death. In England they had heard that workmen have their special laws, their ten hours' bill, their mill inspection, their half timers, and their factory schools, all helping to protect the weak against the strong. No doubt there was much more in London to be seen and heard.

But how were they to make the voyage? They had no money, and no passports. Workingmen in

---

1   (1828 - 1897) . —Ed.

2   Not Eugène but Ernest Edouard Fribourg (1834 - 1903)—the author has misnamed the bronze worker. —Ed.

Paris seldom save, for work is fitful, rent is high, and meat and wine are dear. But Tolain and Fribourg were not common folk. They whispered to their fellows that a great occasion offered, and that some one should be sent to London who had eyes and ears, and could observe the state of things among those allies, who had now become their rivals in so many trades. From Belgium, Germany, and Spain, the working men were sending delegates to London. And must France alone be absent from this gathering of the sons of toil? Such failure would be shame and loss for France.

A knot of bronziers held a meeting, and agreed that they would send their delegates to Cromwell Road. A little purse was made of sous—not much, and yet enough; just big enough to pay a third-class fare, and hire a lodging in Soho. M. Tolain and M. Fribourg took upon themselves the rank of delegates from the Paris working men. A passport was applied for in this name of delegates; but the Prefect of Police, M. Boitelle, refused point-blank to sign.

"Delegates of what?" he asked.

"Of a society of working men."

"Societies of workmen are illegal. No association can exist, and no association can appoint a delegate. You must change the law before you ask for passports."

Then the delegates appealed to Cæsar. Napoleon called himself a Socialist—an Imperial Socialist; and he was eager, when he found it safe, to show

Symphorien Boittelle,
Prefect of Police

Napoleon III

himself a friend and patron of all trade societies which turned men's thoughts to social operations and away from barricades.

Prince Napoleon was in London, an Imperial delegate, and this great stir and study of the toiling millions might be turned by him to good account. So Cæsar signed to M. Boitelle, and then the Prefect, under protest, gave the necessary pass.

"You are to know," that functionary said to Henri Tolain, "that this paper is a special one, the bounty of his Majesty, who is above the law. I give you my assurance that if I were master, nothing of this kind should be done in France."

Henri Tolain

Prince Napoléon-Jérôme Bonaparte

CHAPTER III

Barbary Pirates

enri Tolain, chaser in bronze, and Eugène Fribourg, decorative engraver, came to London, where they saw the Prince Napoleon in his state, the English workmen in their shops and yards, the many industries in process, and the nett results in Cromwell Road.

The Prince was very civil, and M. Tolain, as a clever writer (he had sometimes written for the journals, and was known among the Socialist circles), was appointed by the Prince to be reporter to a section of the French Commission,[1] and to send

1   The French Commission was the official body established by

his notes and notions to the Prince. For service in this post, M. Tolain, as a poor man, took his salary, as the richer people took their salaries. He made an excellent report of what he saw, and earned his portion of the public grant as honestly as any other man. But this connection with the Prince, though brief and public, laid him open to attack, and in the sequel led to accusations of his being a secret Bonapartist agent, and the great society he founded a Napoleonic club.

In London, Tolain and Fribourg made acquaintance with three exiles: Hermann Jung, a Swiss watch-maker, George Eccarius, a German tailor, and Eugène Dupont, a French fiddle-maker, who could speak our language, and who knew our working-men. These exiles took the Paris bronziers to the public-houses where our workmen hold their clubs. They met with Odger, Potter, Lucraft, and some others, and were quickly made to see that there is much more practical Socialism in England than in France.

The studious bronziers were amazed; for like all men of French descent they fancied that in every branch of politics and chief of all in social politics—their country holds the torch and bears the flag. In talking with these English friends they learnt that English artisans are paid a higher price for fewer

---

the French government to oversee its participation in the 1862 International Exhibition in London. It was composed of imperial appointees and section leaders drawn from industry, science, and the arts. —Ed.

George Odger

hours of work than French. What is the cause?

"Trades unions are the cause."

"Trades unions? "

"Yes: you have no unions?"

"None," remarked M. Tolain; " such things are unknown in France; the laws forbid them"

"But you represent your trade?"

"Yes, that is true; but only by a special grace. Our trades have no assemblies, presidents, or sec-retaries. All that is dead against the law in France."

Tolain and Fribourg got the rules of English unions; they went to see our co-operative stores; they studied our experiments at Rochdale;[2] and these political Socialists had to own, against their will, that in the practical arts of Socialism they had still some things to learn. When they asked ad-vice about the way of going to work, our work men answered with one voice, "Rely upon yourselves; have nothing to do with Emperors and Ministers; let the working classes look to their own cause."

The two French bronziers went back to their country and their shops, and told their friends what they had seen and heard. A group of sixty working men was formed, in secret, in the Rue des Gravilliers, to study the great social problem set before them. Every one saw that even while

---

2   The 'experiments at Rochdale' refer to the Rochdale Society of Equitable Pioneers, founded in 1844. This pioneering coop-erative of working-class men established principles of demo-cratic control and fair trading that became the foundation of the modern cooperative movement, demonstrating a practical model of worker self-help and economic cooperation. —Ed.

they were studying they must organise their trades. But then the law forbade associations, and the Prefect of Police was not to be approached; for now the year of grace was gone, and France was ruled more sternly than before. Some voices were in favour of appeals to Cæsar, who was known to be coquetting with all social questions; but the English policy of leaning on the toilers, and refusing to accept a patron, had the stronger vote. A clever lawyer, whom they called into their councils, showed them how they might evade the law. While any native society of working men would be illegal, there was nothing in the law to punish members of a foreign society, even though they were French and domiciled in France. This great discovery gave them hope; and, French in genius, they began at once to frame their statutes and propose a fundamental Pact.

The International Exhibition of industrial products had suggested to many persons, to Tolain amongst them, an International Association of industrial producers; and the general sections of that vast collection gave a name and form to the departments of such an organization. If the clever advocate were right, that no law could punish Frenchmen for belonging to a foreign society, his course was clear. The new Society should be foreign—at least in name: it should be English—and its central office on English ground.

The Tuileries were in a doubtful mood. The task on which these bronziers were employed was known to the police; an agent now and then appeared among them in their meetings; and this agent let them see that they might count on high protection if they placed themselves at Cæsar's feet. Of course, they acted with some prudence, for in truth they were not fierce against the Empire, and they chiefly held aloof from it because they felt no confidence that it would last. The Bonapartists were waiting for results, and meant to turn the movement, if they could, into a social crusade, with a Cæsar in its front.

CHAPTER IV

Science and Barricades

olain and Fribourg wrote to London, to inform their English comrades how they stood in Paris, in relation to the masters, and the Empire. They proposed that a society should be formed, consisting of the working classes of all countries— an International Working Men's Association with the English motto—"Everything by the working class" instead of "Everything for the working class." They had been studying in their secret school, and these were the results at which they had arrived. The working man must be redeemed, and his salvation must depend upon himself.

They came to London in September, 1864; their friends had clubbed a franc a month; a purse was made; and the two men, who had conceived and shaped the International in their brains, arrived in Leicester Square. "The brat was born in Paris and has now been sent to nurse in London," said Babal.[1] The English leaders entered on the plan. It was a compliment to them; and as the Frenchmen offered to concede the presidency to Odger, and the secretaryship to Eccarius (the German tailor could speak French), the London workmen were well pleased.

Not so the colony in Leicester Square, the old Republican exiles, whom M. Fribourg calls, with some disdain, the Conscript Fathers of Jacobinism. These political veterans looked on Tolain's mission with distrust. Tolain and Fribourg spoke of politics with a sort of pique, as having proved but vain and sterile studies for the working class. They looked for other agencies of good. They talked of peace, of study, of arrangement, of association. They were dreaming of a golden age, but they were careless under what pavilion it should reign. A better knowledge of each other, a more frequent

---

1   August Bebel (1840 - 1913) had initially opposed socialism, but been won over by the pamphlets of Ferdinand Lassalle, aimed at popularising the ideas of Karl Marx (although, privately, Marx made unkind remarks about Lassalle). Bebel had been made susceptible to these ideas by difficulties he had encountered as an itinerant carpenter in early life and possibly by his being rejected as physically unfit to serve in the Prussian army. The Italian army had also rejected him. —Ed.

August Bebel

interchange of thought, a clearer view of the great laws which govern rise and fall in wages, and a means of stretching friendly hands from town to town, from sea to sea, in case of need these are the ends we have in view, they urged; not secret plots and wine-shop agitation, with a view to barricades, to bloodshed, and to change of kings for emperors and emperors for kings. But Percy Street and Leicester Square were not appeased.

"Plon-plonians!"[2] cried the exiles, flushed with rage; "these rogues are bought and sold; the traitors, they have touched his silver; they are lost to shame. Avoid them, honest men!"

In Percy Street, just round the corner out of Rathbone Place, one Monsieur Jacques, an exile, kept a lodging-house and dining-room of humble sort, at which more history was made than in a score of palaces and halls of state. Here patriots of all nations, who had lost their fine estates, and had to sup on fifteen-pence, including beer and pipes, assembled of an evening, ate their pottage, cast their scraps of news about, and sang their revolutionary songs. It was a house worth noting well, the Golden Ball in Percy Street, then kept by Monsieur Jacques, a handy cook, a nimble host, and generous friend. Jacques had a little fortune of his

---

2   A reference to Prince Napoléon Jerôme Bonaparte's well-known soubriquet, Plon-Plon. Two theories exist regarding the soubriquet: one, that it stemmed from the difficulty he had as a child in pronouncing his own name; the other, that he earned it by fleeing from battle when bombs fell. —Ed.

own, but many of his lodgers could not pay their rent and table fare. The man was liked, and men renowned in letters, such as Louis Blanc and Victor Schoelcher, have been seen with him; but bit by bit his fortune slipped from his control; he had to sell the Golden Ball to pay his debts, and he is now in Paris, lost in the great revolutionary crowd. But while he kept the Golden Ball it was the home of all lost causes, of all compromised and disaffected men. When the Napoleons reigned in Paris, the Republic reigned in Percy Street; and when the Bonapartes were expelled from France and a Republic was proclaimed at the Hôtel de Ville, there was a counter proclamation of the Commune at the Golden Ball. Beneath the roof of Monsieur Jacques the fate of France is always in the scale. To-day it is the Monarchy, tomorrow the Republic, and the next day, perhaps, the Empire. Everything that is—is wrong. The Golden Ball is but a counterpart of the Hôtel de Ville.

In Percy Street the famous list of members of the Republican Government was framed. In Percy Street the war was opened on the French Society of the Rights of Man. In Percy Street the schism in the Masonic lodges was contrived. In Percy Street the female revolutionary clubs were formed. In Percy Street the Commune, red and revolutionary, was organised. In fact, a permanent conspiracy, of which the names, the members, and the objects change from year to year, is always sitting in a fume of soup, a cloud of smoke. A map of Paris,

Alexandre-Auguste Ledru-Rollin

pricked and stained, is on the board; above which leans a line of bearded chins, intent on raising barricades (of paper) at controlling points, from Père la Chaise to Point du Jour.

Between such refugees as used the house of Monsieur Jacques, in Percy Street, and the two delegates from the Rue des Gravilliers, who had come to study work and wages in a year and festival of peace, there was a gap which neither party had the wish to bridge. The exiles, with that yearning of the heart for home which Sydney felt—which dims the vision and distracts the brain—imagined that the Empire was about to vanish of itself; the delegates, with a closer knowledge of existing facts, could see that the Napoleons still had root and strength in France, if not in Paris, Lyons, and Marseilles. Each spoke the language of his time, and neither understood the other. Those who dwelt in London had not changed; like other exiles, they had learnt nothing, forgotten nothing in a dozen years; while those who dwelt in Paris, breathing a more sprightly and mercurial air, had left the dreams of '48 behind them, and engaged their fancies in the chase of newer spirits of the air. They could not judge each other.

"We are near the end," the exiles gasped; "a few weeks, and the barricades go up."

"You live in a fools' paradise," sneered Tolain, you will wait along time for your barricades; and while you wait the workman starves and dies"

When Tolain went to speak with Ledru Rollin,[3] at his villa in St. John's Wood Park, this burly tribune of the people heard him with a smile. What could he know—he, chaser in bronze—of the great laws which bring on revolutions? How could such as he advise? "My friends," the exile answered, "Go your ways; in six months Paris will have risen, the Empire will have past, and the Republic will have been founded by consent of every town in France."

---

3   Alexandre Auguste Ledru-Rollin (1807 - 1874) was a veteran of the 1848 revolution. He had fled to London after being charged with sedition following the failed republican uprising of 1849, but he had maintained his radical contacts and gone on to publish pamphlets and manifestos against Napoleon III, on which basis he was sentenced in absentia to deportation. —Ed.

CHAPTER V

The Master-Mind

A mong the foreigners then in London, to be met from time to time in un-known clubs and public houses, was a man of singular force and fate;—a Hebrew by his blood, a Frenchman by his birth, a German by his schooling, by his family, and by the struggles of his early life. His name was Marx—Karl Marx.

This Marx was born in Trier, the stately city on the Mosel, when that province was a part of France, so that his birth was French, and he can claim at anytime a Frenchman's rights. His father was a Jew—well housed, well read, well off—with a desire, not often found in Jews, to seek distinction in the camp. No Jew could carry arms in Germany in those days, and the elder Marx accepted a career in France. The son is like his sire, a citizen of the world. When Trier was once more German, Marx resumed his native flag. His son was put to school. Karl Marx became a scholar, versed in languages and arts, a doctor of philosophy, a writer and a speaker of repute, an editor with subtle insight, and a prophet of opinions which the world in general, and the radicals in particular, held to be extreme. A paper which he edited in Cologne, *The New Rhine Gazette*, was dreaded by the liberal party more than by the feudal party. Many of the liberals called him a deceiver and betrayer. He was certainly more terrible to his friends than to his foes. For Marx was less of a political reformer than a social prophet. If he hated kings, he hated capitalists even more than kings. A cold, unsmiling man, he would have stripped a Crœsus of his money rather than a kaiser of his crown. He was not a Communist, as Alexander Herzen and Michael Bakouvine were Communists, from Tartar habit and tradition, but from deep and close, if only fitful, speculations of his own.

With Blind, with Freiligrath, and other learned men, he came to London, where he lived in great obscurity and poverty, no one knew how. He never entered our society, and English men of letters hardly heard his name. He was supposed to write no little for the foreign press, not only German,

Karl Marx

Alexander Herzen

but American and French. A man of various learning, he could turn his pen to some account, but he was more concerned with politics on the Vistula and Neva than with politics on the Hudson and the Rhine. M. Herzen was his friend. Herzen was rich, and had his *Kolokol* to edit, his *Développement des Idées Revolutionnaires en Russie* to compose, and other work to do, in which the press of Rupert Street was much employed. Karl Marx found some employment in these tasks. But he desired to influence, and if need were to destroy. He spent his mornings in the British Museum, poring over rare and opulent tomes; his evenings in the public houses where the trade societies hold their clubs.

It is no secret that this man has high connections in the service—that his wife is the sister of a great minister of state. What causes him to shun the company of his equals is not known. Some say it is no other than ambition—the desire to rule and reign. The doctor is original and special in his views. When Proudhon startled Paris by his essays on what he called the fallacies of Political Economy, Doctor Marx assailed the democratic teacher with a power of logic and a wealth of learning that were keenly felt. For Proudhon hated Communism with all his soul,and in his treatment of this theme (and most of all in his famous chapter, "The Philosophy of Misery") he gave the Hebrew doctor many a chance which Marx was but too quick to seize. In answer to Proudhon's book came out *Das Kapital*, by Karl Marx, in which appeared a little chapter called "The Miseries of Philosophy". Most readers and all writers of the Socialistic school, remember how the veteran Frenchman suffered in this war of words. From that day Marx was noted as a man who might do much—it might be good, it might be evil—but he was not likely to remain a stranger to the intellectual conflicts of our time.

In evil hour the Paris bronziers met this learned and unsmiling Jew.

On the 28th day of September, 1864, a small number of workmen—English, Germans, Polish, French—assembled in a room of St. Martin's Hall, Long Acre, when Professor Beesley took the chair, and Tolain laid his project on the board. A little buzz of talk was heard; some names (as Marx, Eccarius, Odger, Lucraft, Llama, Wolff) were mentioned as a first committee; and a vote was taken on the question that a congress should be held on neutral ground—in Brussels, if it might be in the following year. No great personage was present; it is only guessed that certain persons stood behind the scenes. M. Fribourg calls both heaven and earth to witness that no one of political weight was in the business, either first or last. An English lord proposed to be the patron of the young society, and, like an English lord, he offered to subscribe 10*l.* a year if they would place him at their head. Ten pounds a year was not a sum to be despised; but then the artisans had started with a principle— that of owing their salvation to themselves alone.

Edward Spencer Beesly

They would not have the noble lord for patron, and the noble lord would not subscribe ten pounds a year on any other terms.

Next night there was a tea and dance, in which the Frenchmen joined. Karl Marx was there; and was observed for once—to smile. He had induced these working men, against their wiser judgment, to depart so far from their pacific course of study as to undertake a crusade for the Poles. The icy doctor was observed to smile that night, and while the lighter people waltzed and sang the Marseillaise, he told the wondering artisans that Monsieur Proudhon was a fool.

The workmen stared and laughed. They had not read *Das Kapital*; and were not dreaming that the foreign doctor whom they saw before them was the nameless Cæsar of their cause.

VI

The Fundamental Pact

With Odger president, Eccarius secretary, and offices at No. 18, Greek Street, Soho Square, the International was a fact. Tolain and Fribourg, having spent their poor supply of francs, subscribed in sums of five sous each by their expectant friends, returned to Paris, and reported that the deed was done. The infant born in Paris had been put to nurse on foreign soil. Their money had been wisely spent, and in a few weeks they would see what they would see.

Some six weeks after the meeting at St. Martin's Hall, a letter came from Greek Street to the Rue des

Gravilliers a letter written in the English tongue, and on a common sheet of paper; but this letter was no ordinary scrawl from friend to friend, containing gossip of the hour. It was a new handwriting on the wall. It was the promise of a golden age; it was the summons to a day of wrath. The style was that of Marx. In short, it was a copy of the document by which the International Working Men's Association was to live—a copy of the Fundamental Pact.

A meeting of the Paris brethren was convened in secret to receive this paper; but the use of foreign tongues has been denied to Frenchmen in general, and to Paris workmen in particular, and no one in the room could read the sheet. Then search was made for some one, safe and sure, who could translate the letter into French. But while the group were waiting for a readable copy of the Pact, they formed themselves into a section; framed their statutes (Frenchmen are so quick in framing statutes!), named themselves, in sharp evasion of the law, the Paris Branch of the International Working Men's Association; and appointed Tolain, Fribourg, and Limousin as their corresponding secretaries. When the Pact was written fairly out in French, and read, it was adopted by the group, and ordered to be put in type. In type! But printing is not done by magic. Presses, type, and paper cost much money, and the dreamers in the Rue des Gravilliers had exhausted all their stock of sous. M. Blot, a patriotic printer, was approached. Would he oblige them with a job on credit? Twenty thousand copies of the statutes were required. M. Blot obliged them, and the job was done. When twenty thousand copies of the statutes were in print, and when the press had given them wings, the first part of their task was an accomplished fact. As Fribourg says, "The International Working Men's Association took possession of France."

Possession of France! Without authority from the Emperor and his Prefect of Police? The fact was so; whatever may have been the reason why. The clever advocate who told the workmen that the law could never touch them while they called themselves a foreign body, seemed as though he knew his trade. They took advantage of the doubtful law, and waited for that action of the state which has so often shown itself beyond consideration for the printed codes.

The Paris Branch was opened, No. 44, Rue des Gravilliers, where the secretaries met, and members were enrolled. Two copies of the statutes were addressed to men in power, but only as an act of grace; one copy to M. Boitelle, Prefect of Police, a second copy to M. Rouher, Minister of the Interior—just to let them know that the Paris Branch of the International Working Men's Association kept no secrets. It was wise to send these copies, since the sending of them forced the Government, at least by implication, to declare itself. If nothing should be heard in answer, they could count on toleration, if not more.

M. Boitelle made no sign; M. Rouher made no sign. The workmen read the silence of these Ministers for consent in one of these two forms—either as a confession that the law could not be made to reach them, or as an intentional connivance in a breach of law. Opinion is divided as to which of these alternatives was true, though light has since been shed upon the secrets of that day.

"You should have warned us, if you saw us entering an illegal path," said André Pierre Murat, one of those mechanics whom the Imperial Government put on trial, four years later, for belonging to an illegal society; we inferred from your abstention that our course was lawful. We were not accountable in France for what was being done in London. Had you told us we were wrong, we might have tried to get a more express permission to exist."

The ministers could only urge, in general terms, that they were bound, by high considerations of public order, to adopt a course of watchfulness and expectation towards the new society, and act against it only in the public interest when it had become apparent that the ends proposed were no less dangerous than the means employed.

But whether they were lawful or unlawful, they were soon at work. It was a generous dream; and nearly all the men who joined it, and who gave it hope, were men of peace and study—chiefs and thinkers in their class. Kings send ambassadors to each other's courts, and statesmen hold their congresses from time to time. Why should not working men consult each other on their common interests and their common rights? The sixty members in the Rue des Gravilliers claimed to represent a hundred millions more in Europe, not to count their brethren in Australia, India, and the United States. They were, they said, the men who work and fight. They fell the trees; they till the ground; they reap the harvest; they produce all forms of human wealth. Why should not that which they produce be theirs? "Because" their teachers said, "the labourer is enslaved." Then let the labourer be redeemed. By whom? Himself. No other power, said Marx, can rescue him, for all the classes higher in the scale are leagued against him; not by conscious bonds and forms, but by their special interests in the stored-up capital of the world. From them he has no more to hope. They are his enemies, even though they call themselves his friends. The best of them could not save him if they would, the worst of them would not save him if they could. "If you would be redeemed from slavery," M. Tolain urged in Paris workshops, "you must give up politics as sterile; you must study the great social problems; you must join the Paris branch; you must support the Fundamental Pact"

The cry of this new gospel ran through every part of France.

Henri Martin

CHAPTER VII

First Strife for Power

ome of the best known men in France acclaimed the entry of these work-men on the public stage. Henri Martin, the historian, wrote to the papers that he had read with profound emotion of the meeting at St. Martin's Hall. "We have a feeling that something great has come into the world," he wrote, "and that the hall in Long Acre will become famous in history. We know that the chill of death, which lies on the surface of our society, has not reached the popular heart, and that the sources of our life are not destroyed." Jules Simon, the Academician (now the Minister), was warmer in approval than Henri Martin. He applied for leave to add his name as member to this new society that was to save the world.

Much mystery was made of the affair. The Fundamental Pact was shown to every one in English, signed by Odger, Cremer, and Wheeler; names which Paris lips could not be taught to burr. The card of fellowship was in English too. Each man had a number (as in jails), to which he answered, and by which he could be secretly addressed, even in a public journal. M. Jules Simon bore the number 606, and paid an entrance fee of ten francs.

But though Tolain and his brethren in the Rue des Gravilliers called the Paris section of the International a branch society, and gave their members cards in English to evade the law, they would not suffer Odger, Cremer, and Co. (they hardly thought as yet of Marx) to govern them, or even interfere with what was done in France. Among themselves they recognised the fact which they denied to Boitelle and his agents, that this International Association was a French society, though it had its quarters for the moment on a foreign soil.

A crucial test occurred. Some French Republicans and Socialists, of the Blanqui school, desired to join the Paris section, not as members, but as leaders, saying they could bring with them ten thousand working men. Among these men was Henri Lefort, a well-known journalist, who wished to be appointed Correspondent general of the Association to the press of France, in which capacity he would have

Jules Simon

had the charge of all negociations and communications with the press. The English members thought this offer from Lefort would make their fortunes. No great progress had been made in winning the great journals to their side. The flush of curiosity was almost spent. Few members had of late come in. The hope of holding a public conference, and of making a distinct announcement of their effort, was postponed. They had no money, credit, and connection with the forces which for good and evil rule the world. An offer, therefore, from an able writer, who had friends in every journal office, and who counted in his wake ten thousand working men in Paris only, not to speak of Lyons, Rouen, and Roubaix, was like a god-send to the men in Greek Street. They accepted him, and sent him his credentials as their agent with the papers. But their Paris comrades saw this matter in another light. With them it was a principle to ask no help from those above them in the social scale. Lefort, in such a post as correspondent-general to the press, would be the one man of their body known to all the world. He would be the International—he, an author, journalist, politician, member of the intellectual class! If not their equal, he would be their patron, possibly their master. Tolain and Fribourg, actual founders of the International, could not see themselves despoiled of power. They thought the men in London, who conferred commands so briskly, hardly knew their place; they must be taught a lesson not to interfere in France.

The brethren in the Rue des Gravilliers bitterly complained of Odger, Cremer, and their friends, as not being Radical enough for them. These leaders of the English Unions were behind the age on two great points—on women and the middle class. The Paris workmen have proscribed these branches of society. They have declared that woman has no place in the workshop, in the forum, in the press; that by her nature she is nurse and cook, not student, worker, teacher; that "to man belongs the right to labour and to study problems, while woman rocks the cradle and adorns the workman's house." They have equally declared against the middle class. The middle class has money, education,grace of learning, influence in the world—all things to which they have no grain of natural right. They are usurpers, enemies of the poor, the uncrowned tyrants of the household and the street. A just society would not endure them; they can have no part in a regenerated world; and hence, to ask their help in bringing on the golden age is useless.

Odger and Cremer will not go these lengths. They keep the woman question open, and in public meetings pledge their aid in finding female work, and also, when it may be, female votes. They show no hatred of the middle class as such, but only of an unjust master here and there. In fact, they wish to have the help of all good men in bringing to an issue some of the high social problems which engage their minds. They hold the intellectual classes in the highest honour, and are sometimes tempted

William Randal Cremer

to accept their lead. In Greek Street, therefore, it was held that membership of the society should be open to every one engaged in work, no matter of what kind that work may be—hand-work, brain-work, or a combination of the two sorts. Odger would have let in Raphael, Händel, Dickens; would have let in Grote, Macaulay, and Carlyle. The Swiss and German members were with Odger on this point, for Marx was of the middle class—a doctor of philosophy, a writer and a journalist like Lefort himself. The council, therefore, voted for Lefort.

Tolain refused to recognise this vote. Was London to dictate to Paris? Were the Odgers and the Cremers to appoint a generalissimo for France? In that case, London would assume the whole direction of events. The Paris workmen wrote a letter to Lefort, in which they told him plainly he had no authority to act. "Your repute," they told him, "is a danger, not a benefit, for our cause; and think of you as highly as we may, we will not have you at our side." Lefort was vexed, and feeling sure of Odger and the London conclave, he was rash enough to threaten them with his displeasure. As the Rue des Gravilliers resisted, he appealed to Greek Street for support; but Tolain and Fribourg were too quick for even this experienced revolutionist; for while he sent his message of complaint to London, they put francs into their purses, caught the train and boat, and as the morning broke, they stepped on shore at London Bridge. They first sought out Eugène Dupont, their countryman; and having gained him over to their views, they went with him to Hermann Jung, the Swiss, who was the corresponding secretary for Switzerland. Him, too, they gained; and so the day wore on in private visits, conferences, and successes. Long before the council met, the two Parisians were assured of a majority of votes; and, therefore, when they came into the room in Greek Street, they assumed a lofty tone.

"We, Fathers of the Association," they began, "deny the right of this General Council to interfere in our home affairs; we are free members of a confederation, and so long as we do nothing contrary to our principles we mean to be the masters in our own house" Lefort was absent, and the absent, as our neighbours say, are always in the wrong. Deserted by the foreign members, Odger and his fellows had to cancel their appointment. M. Lefort, the leading journalist of their party, was insulted, and at night the two Parisians took the boat at London Bridge for France.

VIII

Geneva

I n fifty hours, and at a cost of fifty francs a piece, the two Parisians had invaded London, overset a constitution, and deposed a ruling power. They told their section they had conquered; but the victory they had gained was over England and Odger, rather than over the middle classes and Lefort. "In fine," says Fribourg, "the General Council never interfered again with the appointments made by the Paris section." In more certain words, the power of the Association passed to Paris. Odger was the chief in name, but Tolain was become the ruler of events.

A second year elapsed before a congress could be held. Of right, the first of these great gatherings should have been in London, where the council had its seat, and where the mystic idiom of the cards and of the Pact was understood. But such a choice would not have pleased the Paris delegates, already jealous of the fame acquired by London as "the nurse." As Paris was not open, and as Brussels was too near, Geneva offered them the best advantages of site, security, and speech.

In all that touches race and tongue Geneva is a French city, where the manners and the lights are French. She lies on a French river, near the French frontier. On two sides France looks down into her streets. With one hand she can reach to Paris, with the other hand to Lyons; yet the soil is free, the press is open, and the city safe. A red flag floats from every tower, a dozen cafés line the quays, and every man who sips his kirsch and swills his beer can write and speak his mind without the dread of spies.

It suited Paris that the first great public conference should be held in a French-speaking town, for since the "brat" was French by birth, it was of moment that the speeches and the rules should be in French, and that the prominence which London had acquired in the movement should be lessened by pacific means. In London, English would have had a preference, while German and Italian might have had a chance. George Odger, president of the Association, would have sat as president of the congress, and the leaders in the movement might have been the Cremers, Lucrafts, and their friends. Instead of France appearing in the front and at the head, she would have figured as a province only— she, the parent of this great idea! So Geneva was selected, and the English were deposed from leadership by what appeared a natural cause and necessary process, their incompetence in the affair of French.

In the Route du Chêne, one Treib, a German, keeps a brasserie for artisans: a simple man, who sells good beer, and smiles on every thirsty cause in turn. He is no politician, Treib, but one who keeps his shop, and finds as usual that his shop keeps him. Some sixty delegates arrived and held their meetings in this brasserie of the Route du Chêne. They spoke all tongues, from Russ to Spanish, but the three great idioms of the world prevailed, and it was evident to all that some one must preside who would be able to exhort the speakers, whether English, French, or German, in their several tongues. Now came the question, who was master of these lingoes? Not the English deputies; not the French deputies. Karl Marx was absent from the congress; he detested congresses; and he has never shown himself since that eventful day when he had walked into St. Martin's Hall—and smiled. A man was found in Hermann Jung, the Swiss watchmaker, who was master of these idioms, and a knowledge of these idioms made him master of the situation. He was seated in the chair.

This chair was like a throne—a seat of thorns; for Jung soon found that he could order this and that, but had no power to make men do his will. A dozen speakers rose at once; this man in French, that man in German, and another man in Russ. Jung could not put them down. "What!" cried the fiery zealots, "have we come together to redeem the world, and, having come so far, must we keep silence in the Route du Chêne? Forbid it all the rules of heaven and earth!" Another evil met him at the door. The London council had, it seemed, abused the right of issuing invitations, and the Paris deputies protested with much force against this stretch of power. Among the persons who had been invited by the London council were some students of the Quartier Latin; Protot (afterwards so busy in the civil war), Humbert, Carlavaz, and others, who appeared in the Route du Chêne, and took their seats. Protot got up at once, and, in a fiery speech, proposed to turn the congress into an attack upon the Empire and the Bonapartists. For a while the English listened to his eloquence, not catching easily his aim; but the Parisians shouted to him, screamed at him, rushed upon him, and at length expelled him from the house. Fierce words were uttered in this struggle. "Down with him! pitch him into the lake!" Herr Treib was fearful lest his house should come about his ears.

CHAPTER IX

In the Route du Chêne

he Opinions of Paris were adopted in a formal manner as the Principles of the Association. So says M. Fribourg in as many words. This compliment was due to Paris—first for her pre-eminence in the world of thought, and then as being the parent of the new society. Her members asked for this submission as her due; for this poor Paris, now so broken and deserted, has been spoiled by flatterers on the largest scale and in the warmest phrase. A year since only, Victor Hugo told a mob who came to draw his chariot through the streets (a common cab, two francs an hour, with twopence for a pot of beer) that the smoke of Paris furnished all the rest of Europe with ideals, lights, and inspirations. Thanks to rhapsodists like Hugo, Paris is not blind to her own merits, and when all the trades were going to meet in Geneva and inaugurate a golden age, it had been felt that Paris should be represented at the congress by an overwhelming force of votes, in case of either London or Geneva setting up a rival claim to lead the working men.

A fund had been subscribed to pay expenses; men of eminence had lent their names and given their francs; among the rest Jules Simon, now a Minister of the Republic, sent in twenty francs. A goodly sum was raised, and sixteen members of the Paris Branch repaired to Switzerland from Paris, Lyons, and Rouen; not less than eleven from the Rue des Gravilliers; not to speak of Protot, Humbert, and the other students from the Quartier Latin, who appeared by invitation of the London council; not to speak of Blanqui, Tridon, and a group of revolutionary Socialists, who came unbidden to the Route du Chêne. No perfect list of those who took their seats has been preserved; in fact, the row, which deepened more than once into a riot, caused the papers to be torn and lost. The delegates from England were too few to be forgotten in a crowd. In all they were but four; and two of these were men of foreign name and birth. Odger and Cremer represented English views and interests; while the other two delegates, who signed and spoke for London—George Eccarius, a German tailor, and Eugène Dupont, a French musical instrument maker-had no objection to the Opinions of Paris being adopted as the Principles of the Association.

A foreign artisan, though he may live in London, has a natural sympathy for France. France is to him the country of ideas, of equality, of social changes and experiments, of which his class takes note as pathways leading towards the golden age. Unhappily, too, the English delegates were weak in what was now of primary concern—the article of foreign speech. Dupont spoke French; Eccarius, French and German; but they were not natives of the soil. They shared in Victor Hugo's views about the smoke of Paris being light to all the world. These circumstances put the English members at a disadvantage. Out of sixty delegates they counted only two in a division. Then the views of London were not only less heroic, dreamy, and fantastic than the views of Paris, but these English views were urged with the degree of moderation and reserve which clings to men of practical genius, even in their wildest flights. Such caution was unpopular in the Route du Chêne, where an opinion to be relished by the workmen must be frothy, like the beer. Treib knows his customers, and never serves them with a mug of drink until the liquor foams into ahead. The English oratory rarely foamed.

Before the meeting was convened, a circular had been sent from London, with a list of subjects to be studied and debated in the Route du Chêne.

Johann Georg Eccarius

They were twelve in number. 1. Organization of the society: its objects and its means of action. 2. Working men's societies: their past, present, and future; holidays; strikes, and the means of preventing them; primary and professional instruction. 3. Work of women and children in mills, considered from a moral and a sanitary point of view. 4. Reduction in the hours of work; the obligation of work for all. 5. Association, principle, and application; cooperation. 6. Relation of labour and capital; foreign competition; treaties of commerce. 7. Direct and indirect taxation. 8. International institutions, mutual credit, paper money, weights and measures, coins, and languages. 9. Necessity of reducing the power of Russia in Europe by extending the principle of the right of people to dispose of themselves, and by the reconstitution of Poland on a socialistic and democratic base. 10. Standing armies, in relation to production. 11. Religious ideas: their influence on social, political, and intellectual movements. 12. Establishment of a society for mutual help; support of orphans.

If we drop the article about reducing Russia by the check of a socialistic republic in Warsaw—a fantastic article inserted by Karl Marx against the better judgment of the working men—what is there in this list of subjects to be feared? These subjects are debated in every club and cottage, and at every congress of learned men. In No. 4, a corner of the veil is lifted, where the Congress was invited to pronounce a verdict on the question of obligatory work for all. Yet this is not a theme to shirk. Some great philosophers have written on it; many churches have adopted it; and the whole scheme of life implies it. "He who will not labour, neither shall he eat." If sages and divines may preach the doctrine of universal labour, working men may surely study it without offence.

CHAPTER X

French and English

In studying these high problems London and Paris took their several ways. Each wrote a memoir on the subject; that of London was a memorandum, that of Paris was a treatise. Tolain came into the brasserie with a roll of paper big enough to contain a book; and this great roll of paper he proposed to read. Here were the Opinions of Paris, edited in the Rue des Gravilliers. Odger, with the weight of his authority as president, proposed to give the conference a practical turn, to stop the flow of talk, and rush at once into the Nine Hours' Bill and strikes. The English members wanted deeds, not phrases. Tolain, as a Frenchman, could not see the difference. To a Frenchman words are facts. "What can we do," he asked "except prepare and read our memoirs?" All that reading would do little good, the English thought; for English workmen are not formal, logical, precise. "We must lay down our principles, declare our objects, and define our limits," urged the French; "we must concoct our rules, and give the world some reason why we claim to live! " All that, the English thought, might be assumed without much blare of trumpets; for an English artisan cares little for ideas in the abstract, and still less for flowers of speech; but he is keen enough about the wrongs which gall his shins and touch his belly. "What a sorry beast it is this Bull," the Frenchmen sniffled in the Route du Chêne; "Look! no ideas, no syntheses, no imagination! He will never light the torch and lead the world. He cannot grasp the noble, the devoted, the sublime. You talk to him of a generalization, and he thinks you mean a man with feathers in his cap and mounted on a showy horse!" These men of grand ideas took much trouble with their comrades from the Thames. John Bull has hardly any soul for things which drive Jean Crapaud frantic with delight. He cannot feel fraternal, like his brother in Villette. He has no solidarity, as solidarity is understood in France. Much effort is required to make him international. He is not moved by systems, and the finest diagnosis leaves his heart untouched. To talk to him of "radical and universal harmonies of interest," is to speak in unknown tongues.

"What would you have?" the Frenchmen asked these practical delegates from London. Have! A nine hours' bill; in time an eight hours' bill; and higher rates of wages for their work. Here much debate occurred; and many choppes of beer were drunk; the Switzers not being used to this conception of a right of labour limited by law.

"You would not take away my right to labour when and where I please?" puts in a Genevese.

"We would; at least in shop and mill; at home you might defy our rules."

"You would restrain my liberty to sell my time and skill?"

"We would"

"You would! Then I, for one, should snatch my rifle up. You make no laws for me."

"No man should be a slave—not even if he likes to be one."

"But observe the rule in our free cantons," said the Switzer. " Here the people govern; all the men have arms, and all the young ones are at school; yet in this democratic country, where no princes breathe the air, no patrons pack the Chambers, every man is free to sell his labour where he pleases, just as much and just as little as he likes."

"That method would not suit us."

"You could not, in your country, leave the workmen free to bargain with their patrons, each man for himself, without the aid and the restraint of law?"

The Congress could do no such thing. "To leave the labourer and the capitalist free to bargain with each other," said the English delegate, was to leave a lambkin free to make what terms he liked with a wolf. The labourer would have no chance." It might be otherwise in other places—in the mills of Winterthur and in the weaving sheds of St. Gallen; but a hundred Swiss examples of free trade in labour would not help a Sheffield cutler and a Bolton spinner to improve his lot.

The English stuck to what they called the point, in spite of Tolain's pleas for universal progress and the ultimate redemption of the working class. "If you would have the International Association thrive in England, you must show that it can help the workman in his need. Unless some proof is given of practical utility no success can be expected on the English soil."

What would the English have? Two things at least. A clear announcement, to be followed by supporting action, in behalf of shorter hours of labour and a higher rate of wages. What was meant by action in support of such announcement? Would they have the International Association interfere with strikes? Of course they would. Why not? To sanction strikes was the main business of the body; all the rest was dust and chaff. If the trades must help them they must help the trades.

"You sacrifice the future," cried the French; "But we shall gain the present," urged the English,"and the present day is that in which we have to live."

CHAPTER XI

Opinion of Paris

Monsieur Tolain read his roll of paper, taking many hours to read it; and, supported by his sure majority, he got it passed, although the English and German delegates withheld their votes.

It was a general statement, with a preface, a preamble, and nine sections, treating capital and labour, education and the family, co-operation, holidays, and strikes, taxation, standing armies, free trade and treaties of commerce, religious ideas, and the reinstitution of Poland.

"Of all the phases which humanity has assumed, no phase, in our opinion, has been more important than that on which the people have now entered. Up to this time the people have not really existed. In the most solemn acts of social and political life, democracy, even when it seemed to be following its own ideas, has been led about by the employers, and one has lately seen the strugglers fighting for a choice of tyrants." There were fifty pages of such stuff; elaborate definitions of capital and labour, of the objects of instruction, of the military power, and of the true philosophy of trade. "Work," said the dreamers of the Rue des Gravilliers, "is the act by which man appropriates to himself the powers of nature, and transforms her first fruits into his own substance." Not much use, the English thought, in all these phrases! "Capital is the sum of things produced and not consumed, destined by their creator, either to assist in future production, or provide against such eventualities as sickness, age, and loss of strength." How will that help us, thought the English, to an eight hours' bill?

The chief Opinions of Paris, then and there adopted as the Principles of the International Association, may be stated in a few lines—

No interest to be charged for money lent.

No obstacles in the way of free exchanges.

No one shall refuse to work.

No public schools; no gratuitous and compulsory education.

Liberty for any one to teach.

A common rule for all co-operative societies.

Study much before a strike.

Direct taxation.

An armed people; no professional troops.

Every one may pray as he likes, so long as he is just and moral, and does not bring "his God" into the workshop and the auberge.

Nothing to do with the Polish question. (Here a blow at Marx.)

The roll containing these suggestions has sixteen signatures, beginning with Bourdon, engraver, and ending with Aubry, lithographer. Of course it bears the names of Tolain and Fribourg, founders of the Association. Varlin and Bourdon signed a separate paper, called Opinions of the Minority, of a more decided Communistic tinge. A new colour, one might say a new constitution, was given to the society by this report. The Frenchmen were supported by the Switzers, and the English and German delegates were both out-voted and out-talked. Without repudiating politics, the London delegates kept pretty clear of party questions; but the Paris delegates, though strictly urging that the working men must stand aloof from kings and ministers, were always tending to political action. Blanqui assailed them as a group of Bonapartists in disguise. Would they be tolerated in the Rue des Gravilliers, if M. Rouher had no use for them? He called them agents; they denounced him as a madman. In Geneva, where the workmen knew and liked him, Blanqui was strong, and there was talk about the quays of marching on the Route du Chêne and dipping all these babblers in the lake.

Louis-Auguste Blanqui

For Blanqui shared the views of Percy Street, in London. This society of working men, professing to be non-political, and prating of a revolution to be made in peace, was in his way.

"These fellows will postpone the barricades," he said.

"We shall," they answered; we shall make men happy."

"Then they will not fight. If you divert them from their faith—the worship of a social and democratic republic—they will sink into beasts of burden."

"If their homes are cheery, and their children fed and taught, why should they go into the streets and fight? What would they gain? What they might lose we know their health, their work, and, per-haps, their lives. What would they gain, except a tyrant with a newer name?"

A test of their fidelity occurred. Garibaldi came to Geneva, on his way to Lausanne, where he was going to preside over the Congress of Peace. To-masi, delegate from Bologna, made a motion that a deputation should be named to wait upon the General and invite him to attend the congress. Tolain opposed this motion, on the ground that Garibaldi was a politician, and that they had nothing to do with politics and political men. He proposed, as an amendment that the congress, while it rendered every just and proper homage to the character of Garibaldi, as well as to his perfect honour, held that it was no part of the business of artisans to run after a citizen, however illustrious he might be

Giuseppe Garibaldi

that if the General, who was already president of several working men's societies in Italy, had chosen to take his seat in the congress he would have been received with all the sympathy to which he had a right—that since he had not come amongst them of his own free choice, it was an act of needless deference to send him any invitation to attend. Tolain pressed his motion with such ardour, and was backed by so many French delegates, that the proposition was withdrawn. Garibaldi passed the insult without notice; but he was, and is, a stranger and an enemy of the International Working Men's Association.

At last the meeting ended with a little fête. Geneva is extremely fond of fêtes, to which her quays and streets, and her abounding waters, lend themselves beyond all cities in the world. *Le Chablais*, one of the steamboats plying on the lake, was hired, adorned with flags, provided with a band of music. All the delegates were present, and a crowd of Genevese, who had been staring, laughing, and exclaiming at the congress for a week, were gathered on the Quay des Bergues, and on the Place du Rhône. The flags of many nations, English, French, Italian, German, floated from the ropes. One mast alone was bare—the main. A band struck up; the steamer glided from the port; a shout arose on every side, and with that cry a flag ran up the mast. It was the Swiss flag, but without the cross!

Instead of the white cross appeared these words:

No rights without duties,
No duties without rights.

The flag itself was red, and as the breeze un-curled and swept it forward, many of the citizens who stood on bridge and quay turned pale with anger and alarm. A hundred voices cried at once, "It is the Red Republic they proclaim!"

CHAPTER XII

In France

The flag was up the blood-red flag—the flag of Schwyz, but with the grand omission of the Cross. The instinct of the Genevese was right. That flag without the cross, democracy without religion, was a sign; and as *Le Chablais* steamed away into Lake Leman towards the Savoyard side—a French boat, bound for a French harbour—there is little wonder that the gentry of the Rue des Granges, the merchants of the Quay des Bergues, the tradesmen of the Place du Rhône, should curse the foreign vessel with its foreign freight and foreign flag.

The French police were watching this affair with all the fuss and weakness which had marked their ways for twenty years. M. Boitelle had no orders. Men of the Imperial family were known to look on these reformers of society with favour, and the Emperor himself seemed more and more inclined to lean on them against the middle class. M. Rouher kept his counsel. The society was fighting for him and his master in a hundred ways; not only by dividing the Liberal votes of Paris and by separating class from class, but by withdrawing men's attention from the Empire to the work-room, from the minister to the master, from the question of a dynasty to that of a nine hours' bill. M. Tolain, though he had not meant such service, was dividing the great party of the revolution into hostile camps; the camp of revolutionary Socialists and the camp of revolutionary politicians. He was weakening Blanqui's influence in the streets. He was loosening Favre's interest in the clubs. He was opening an attack upon the Irreconcileables, as a set of old fogies who could not understand the times in which they lived. Not only in the workshops but the press he fought M. Rouher's battles. Chief among the Liberal papers was the *Siècle*, a journal of the middle class, of pure Republican opinions, and, until the *Temps* divided its authority, the most thoughtful organ of the commonwealth in France. This journal, which was hated by Imperialists for its ability and moderation, was denounced by the International Association as the foremost enemy of the working men. All means were taken to decrease its sale. No cabaret, no brasserie, no restaurant used by working men was suffered to take it in, and both in Paris and the provinces the keepers of all houses of public entertainment received a warning not to touch the unclean thing. The Garibaldi incident in the Route du Chêne was highly relished at the Tuileries, for Garibaldi was a demigod in Paris workshops; and a body representing labour made what seemed to be a common cause with the Imperialists against the man of Aspromonte. That refusal of M. Tolain to invite the General to Geneva may have had some influence in deciding France to crush him at Mentana, when he marched on Rome.

M. Boitelle, left without instructions from his master, took a singular and dangerous course. Not daring to arrest M. Tolain and the delegates from the Rue des Gravilliers, lest some secret purpose of the palace should be crossed, yet anxious to secure good evidence of what the congress had been doing at Geneva, he gave orders to arrest the foreign members as they passed through France. These members were arrested, and their papers seized. Unluckily for M. Boitelle, two of these men, Odger and Cremer, were of English birth, and, English like, they made a row about this insult to their country and their flag. Lord Cowley took the matter up; the men were set at liberty; but their papers were detained by the police; and months elapsed before the delegates received them back.

Napoleon was in deep distress, for Königgrätz had placed a rival in the field, whose growth he could not brook, and yet whose power he dared not brave. He wished to please Lord Cowley and to win the working men of Paris. So M. Rouher yielded up the documents to Odger, and requested Bourdon, as the man whose signature stood first on the Paris memoir, to honour him with a call.

M. Bourdon, an engraver, meeting in the Rue des Gravilliers, went to Geneva, like the others, with the sum of 120 francs in his pocket for expenses. He had travelled in a slow train, in a third-class waggon; he had lived in a cheap lodging, fed on humble fare; he was no speaker, writer, soldier; nothing but a toiling man; and yet his trip to Switzerland, with the pure accident of his having been the first to sign the memoir, had conducted him to the cabinet of an all-powerful Minister-Sous-empereur, the clubbists called him—for a conference on equal terms, as Power with Power.

CHAPTER XIII

A Private Interview

"Y ou wish," M. Rouher said to the engraver from the Paris Branch of the International, "to circulate in France the memoir read in Geneva?"

"Yes; it is refused admittance at the frontier town."

A copy of the memoir lay on the Minister's desk; it had been closely scanned, and some few notes were visible on the margin.

"Let us look at this together," said M. Rouher. "Here is an expression to be softened; here is an opening for some words to be inserted. I invite you to consider these expressions, and to make some alteration in the form."

M. Bourdon seized his chance of telling the great Minister what he thought on several things-the rights of labour, the abuse of capital, the sterility of middle-class ideas, the necessity for social changes, the absurdity of wages, and the like; in fact, to preach in the Ministry of the Interior a sermon on the general principles of the International. M. Rouher listened with benignant smiles. To these announcements he had no objections to suggest. He could not say they had no right to entertain such views, and put them forward in the press whenever they could do so lawfully. His observations only touched the point of form.

"How can we change the form and not the sense?" said Bourdon. "We put our thoughts in words, the nearest that occur to us, and we should find it difficult to repeat our thoughts in any other words."

"Well, if that is so," the Minister replied, you force me to maintain the interdiction. Let us see if we can understand each other. You desire to circulate this memoir—could you not insert some words of thanks to the Emperor, who has done so much for the working classes ?"

The engraver told the Minister that the International was not a political body, with the right to either flatter or abuse great persons and great parties; it was only a society to study social problems, and to publish the results of study, leaving every

Eugène Rouher

one to act according to his wants. M. Rouher shook his head. The Emperor must be recognised and thanked for services to the working men; if not, the memoir should not circulate in France.

Bourdon retired to tell his friends in the Rue des Gravilliers the price of Rouher's favour. Tolain could not make the change; and thus the memoir, free to pass in Brussels and Geneva, was condemned in Paris and Lyons to appear as a clandestine piece.

While Bourdon was parleying with the Imperial Minister, Tolain and Fribourg were forming the Paris bureau, which they organised with all the logic and authority of a Jacobin club. Their code consisted of eighteen articles. Art. 1. To be admitted as a member a man must prove his quality of artisan. Art. 5. The subscription is fixed at two sous a week. Art. 11. No credit shall be given to a member in arrear with his subscription. Art. 15. The committee of administration, fifteen in number, chosen by direct suffrage for a year, shall choose their correspondents, cashiers, and archivists. Art. 18. Any false statement of name, age, residence, and trade shall exclude a man; also any arrear of subscription; also any hostility to the principles of the Association. When the bureau was formed, Tolain and Fribourg were appointed correspondents; Louis Eugène Varlin, a bookbinder, was associated in their labours. Jean Pierre Héligon, old book-seller, was named cashier; Félix Eugène Chemalé, a builder's clerk, was made secretary-general. Bourdon took charge of the books and papers of the Paris Branch.

Debates soon rose in Paris on the principles laid down in the Route du Chêne. As usual there was much exaggeration in the matter. Papers like *La Presse* denounced the International to public justice, and a writer in *La Liberté* declared in answer that this young society was a power. Already, while the Association only numbered some few hundreds—most of them in great arrear of pence—these journals counted their adherents by the million, and imagined that they had the banks of London, Amsterdam, and Paris at their back. The Blanquists followed them with calumnies, for Blanqui could not understand a working-class society that was not bent on barricades. The prudence of the bureau was mistaken for subservience to the ruling powers.

The principles of the society were such as tended to preserve the public peace. But little favour was, at first, exhibited to men on strike. The working men were taught to look for nobler changes than a rise in wages and a diminution of the hours of work—a transformation of the rights of labour, and a full redemption of the working man. These phrases helped to keep the Paris masons at their trade; a service of immense importance to the Emperor and his officers at the Hôtel de Ville. A strike of the bronziers of Paris was conducted, on the whole, with so much moderation, and such perfect success against the patrons, that the Prefect of Police invited the trade delegates who arranged the strike to come and see him in his cabinet, where he received them with politeness, and congratulated them on the dignity and firmness they had shown in the affair.

Some incidents occurred in this bronziers' strike, of which the Prefect of Paris had, no doubt, a full report. To give the strike an air, the bronziers sent three members of their body—Valdun, Kin, and Camelinat—to London, in company of M. Tolain and M. Fribourg, founders of the International, as vouchers and introducers of the deputation to their English brothers in Soho. These workmen were to seek support in Greek Street, which was not expected to be material so much as moral. They were well received in club and public-house; they got no end of promises; but the founders of the International said on their return to France, they got but little else. The English workmen had no money to bestow. And yet this visit to Soho had some results. The Paris masters heard of it, and got alarmed, for a mysterious dread of what the London trades could do by way of raising funds had run through Paris, and the press gave wings to any fiction on that subject, if the details were absurd enough to point a sarcasm and provoke a stare. A trades' union was supposed to have unlimited credit with the London banks.

The manufacturers of Paris were divided as to what was best for them to do; some patrons wished to hear of terms; the Government was anxious for the strike to end. The timid masters called a meeting of their trade at Ménilmontant, to compare opinions on the strike, and see if an arrangement could be made. While this assembly was in progress, some declaring for a compromise with the men, and some against it, letters came by post from London, which were opened in full sitting and before the public gaze. A number of bank notes fell out, each note for a thousand francs. It was a shower of wealth, sent over from the English unions as an earnest of their sympathy, a pledge of their support. This opportune arrival turned the tide. "The Bank of England stands behind them," cried the masters, "let us hasten to make terms before our trade and capital are gone." So terms were made, the masters ceding what the bronziers asked—not only fewer hours of work, but higher wages for restricted time; and then the Imperial Prefect sent for Valdun and his fellows to congratulate them on the way in which they had played and won their game.

In those days there was nothing an Imperial Prefect feared so much as strikes; for strikes not only interfere with public order, but compel the officers of state to take a side. To take a side is loss of strength; and hitherto the Government had played to both extremes of French opinion; here defending order, saving society, protecting moral interests; there coquetting with the revolution, professing sympathy for the proletariat, and practising Socialism on the largest scale. A strike compelled the Government to take a side, to compromise itself with one opinion, and it therefore feared and hated strikes. A man who could prevent a strike was worth to the Imperialists a regiment of Guards.

CHAPTER XIV

Service to the Empire

he International repaid the Prefect of Police for shaking hands with Valdun. In a week or so the tailors of the fashionable quarter struck, and came to ask the Rue des Gravilliers for assistance. Tolain would not hear them; strikes were not his means of action; they were English, practical, and compromising; while his notion of a workman's duty was to wait for grander transformations of the social state. These fashionable tailors, dressing the fine people of the Maison Dorée and the Jockey club, showed no fraternal sympathy with the slop-men of the Rue du Temple, who were toiling night and day for crusts of bread. Nor were these tailors on his books; no cards of membership had been secured by them; no weekly payments of two sous had been sent in by them; no member of the International Association had been invited to their managing committee; and, what was worse, that scenic business of the letter and the shower of bank—notes dropping from the clouds upon a wavering meeting, could not be repeated once a week. The snips were left to fight alone, and having neither brains nor cash, they soon gave way. As Fribourg says, "they failed for lack of material resources and moral support" No doubt. Each tailor turned to the companionship of his goose a sadder and a thinner man. The Prefect joyfully reported to M. Rouher that this strike was at an end.

A more important service to the Government was rendered by M. Tolain and his fellow-correspondents in the strike at Roubaix, where the weavers smashed the looms, set mills on fire, and injured those who would not join them in their evil work.

The cause of all this rage was some improvement in the looms, which gave the owners better work from fewer hands, together with some rule or rules not palatable to the weavers. When the men had first objected to the new machines, the master had, unhappily, sent for the police; and these officious gentry took (as their expressive idiom says) the devil by his tail. The devil would not stand his tail being pulled, and factory folk feel sore when the police rush into them and break their heads.

These Roubaix mill-hands struck their work; they fought with the police; they smashed the looms; they fired the factories; they set upon and wounded all who would not help them. They appeared to have been studying in the school of Sheffield. Many of these rioters were arrested; Lille was full of soldiers, prisoners, and police; the frontier was disturbed along the line; and Government was deeply moved by an event which, take what course it might, was sure to bring it loss of power.

The International came forward to condemn the movement in express and general terms. A proclamation issued from the Rue des Gravilliers, in which are found these words:—

"The International Association calls the attention of working men in every country to the fact that the employment of machinery in manufactures raises an economical problem which should be studied at once. We working men recognise the right of working men to an increase of wages when a new machine enables them to produce more." No great harm in such an abstract proposition, prefects of Police would think. Then came the pith and marrow of their proclamation. "Workmen of Roubaix,—Whatever cause of complaint you may have, nothing can justify the acts of which you have been guilty. Believe us, the machine, the instrument of production, should be sacred in your eyes. Believe us, acts of violence compromise your cause, and that of every artisan. Believe us, you are supplying arms to all the enemies of liberty and all the

Félix Pyat

calumniators of working men." This sharp rebuke was signed by Tolain, Fribourg, and Varlin, "on behalf of the Parisian Commission." It was worth an army in the North of France.

All these civilities and services between the Government and the International roused once more the cry of Bonaparte intriguers, of Prince Napoleon's agents, and supplies of money from some secret fund. No one believed that the bank notes showered upon the Ménilmontant meeting came from Greek Street. Where must they look for the true source of these supplies? "The Palais Royal," cried the Blanquists; "creatures of Plon-plon; traitors to the people! Down with them! "

A scene occurred in London on a rainy day in March (1867), of which the Prefect of Police no doubt had full accounts. That he would forward every detail of this story to the Tuileries we may be sure.

One of those exiles of December '51, who used to sup with Monsieur Jacques, in Percy Street, a Capitaine François Clovis Hémont, died in his poor lodging, and his friends in misery wished to honour his remains with an interment such as one may witness every day in Père la Chaise. As Félix Pyat, one of the most eminent of the many revolutionary leaders, was in London (taking care of Félix Pyat, who was then much wanted by the Prefect of Police), they begged the orator to meet them at the captain's grave and sing the customary praises of the dead. Pyat refused this sacred office. He was tired; the weather was unsettled; and the sort of thing was overdone. He would not come. When Tolain, Fribourg, and the three bronziers from Paris heard that their old comrade was to be buried next day in his foreign grave, their hearts warmed up with the old revolutionary fire. They sent to say they would attend, not only in their persons, but as deputations from the Paris trades. When Pyat heard this news, he changed his mind, prepared a revolutionary speech, and met the five Parisian representatives at the captain's grave. A shower of rain was falling on the grass; but the revolutionary leader took his stand beside the open grave, and in a fiery speech exhorted all those present to follow in the footsteps of their dead brother-hating tyrants, loving lowly men, and fighting despots to the last. Then fixing his eyes on Valdun, Camelinat, and Kin, the three bronziers, and on Tolain and Fribourg, the two founders of the International, he explained the missions which had been reserved for them. He spoke of the late congress in Geneva; of the *Social Contract* written by Rousseau; and of the land which owed her freedom to the peasant and the working man. "My fellow-citizens, my fellow-patriots!" he exclaimed, "the cap of Gessler crowns the edifice! I shall rest in peace, even on a foreign soil, if with the book of Jean Jacques Rousseau you have brought back with you to France the bolt of William Tell." The exiles raised a shout, "Long live the Republic!" To which M. Pyat answered, "Yes; long live the Republic!"

Zéphyrin Camelinat

Tolain glanced at Fribourg, in the drenching rain; they glanced at their companions of the bronze works; and they left the grave-yard saying to each other, "If the Citizen Félix Pyat really believes so strongly in the virtues of a poniard, why does he not go and do the deed himself?"

Chapter XV

Fresh Experiments

olain and Fribourg, full of dreams and schemes, were not content with their success as founders of the International Association. In Geneva they had found a city of societies; this lively little canton, with some 80,000 people, having no less than 220 properly organized and registered societies; and they longed to link their names with other noble efforts for the benefit of mankind. They tried to found a bank. They got up a proposal for technical instruction. They formed a League of Peace. They talked of mutual disarmaments. While French diplomatists in Berlin were asking for the left bank of the Rhine, with Mainz, if not Cologne, as compensation for the Prussian victories in Bohemia, while Graf von Bismarck was leading Count Benedetti to commit the one great folly of his life, to write and leave with him, on French official paper, the astounding draft of a secret treaty for the seizure of Belgian soil—the patriots of the Rue des Gravilliers issued an address to the workmen of Berlin, nominally in favour of "peace and liberty," but virtually in favour of the principle of settling questions of public right and law by plebiscites.

"As citizens, no doubt," they said, "we love our mother country [France], but when the spirit of the past [Graf von Bismarck] endeavours to perpetuate prejudices among us, and the adorers of force [King William, General Möltke, and their kith] are trying to revive national animosities, let us workmen not forget that the work in which we have a common interest can only be increased in liberty and peace. There ought to be no question of deciding the nationality of a strip of land [the German Rhine] by force of arms. We should unite our efforts to secure a reign of equity." [So that France might get the Rhine without a blow!) This piece was printed in many languages, and copied into many papers. It was followed by the issue of a circular with this motto, "The chief cause of war is the army," and proposing to effect a great reduction in the forces of all nations by consent of each and all. Lord Clarendon had just put out his scheme of peace, retrenchment, and reform, at

Otto von Bismarck

which the two chief players of the game, the Graf von Bismarck and the Emperor Napoleon, rubbed their palms and smiled. Napoleon met Lord Clarendon half-way; he wanted nothing for himself he said; and only wanted what was just for France. The Rhine was called her natural frontier; not to have that river was a permanent reproach to her; yet he was willing to obtain it without bloodshed, by the free consent of those who owned it. He was ready to disarm. Would Graf von Bismarck give up the "professional militarism"—that was the term by which victorious Prussia was impeached—in which he found his chief delight? While Bismarck paused on his reply, M. Tolain launched his International League of Disarmament a league in which France was represented by Tolain, Fribourg, Chemalé, and three others; England by Stepney, Germany by Schily and Hugo Rothschild, Belgium by Debock, Hungary by Pompiny and Draskulcs, Denmark by Petersen, Russia by Reinfeld, Sweden by Wollin, and Switzerland by Müller. All these men (with one exception, perhaps) were resident in Paris, and had no authority whatever to engage the working classes of their several countries in this Napoleonic league. Yet the effect produced by the announcement was considerable, for the press reported what was said, and left in a mysterious background what was done. "Considering," said the manifesto, "that if, in the actual state of Europe, the freedom, dignity, and independence of nations can have no other guarantee than arms, a national militia offers in case of any acts of aggression better securities for defence than professional militarism."

The working men had taken up the phrase of insult and impeachment. France was then the most "professional" of military powers, while Prussia was, in fact, a country with a "national militia," but the scribes of Paris had been urged to sneer at Germans as a set of rampant martinets in camp and city, whose ridiculous airs were not to be endured by gods and men. This charge of Prussian "militarism" was a set-off to the charge of French "Cæsarism." Cæsarism was a word of evil omen to the working classes, and the Cæsars who disturbed the labour markets by their restless energy were trying to fasten on their rivals in Berlin a more opprobrious name than Cæsarism. "Militarism" suggested troops of Kozaks, prostrate Poland, stalwart Emperor Nicholas, and a stiff parade of armed serfs. M. Tolain, as a representative of labour, flung this phrase of "professional militarism" at the Prussian Court.

So far the Government of the hour was served; its rivals got a dubious name; the Palais Royal and the Tuileries were well content; and having served their purposes this separate league of workmen died.

James Fazy

CHAPTER XVI

Congress of Lausanne

o marked success had been attained as yet by the International in point of numbers and resources. England stood aloof. The sections were in debt. A year after the red flag ran up the main mast of *Le Chablais*, and the bankers of Geneva cried, "It is the Red Republic!" neither London, Brussels, nor Berlin could count five hundred members who had signed their cards and paid their fees. Paris took the lead, in numbers as in other matters, but her books showed something under six hundred members, and instead of having funds in hand to carry on the social war, she owed for rent and printing 466 francs. It was the same elsewhere. Berlin was worse than Paris, Brussels weaker than Berlin. In London the association had no living root. In Florence, Naples, and Milan, workmen looked upon the movement with suspicion, for the workmen were with Garibaldi heart and soul, and Garibaldi was no friend of the International. The General Council were not able to print a news sheet of their own. Geneva had no more to show than other cities. There were sections, officers, generals, but the money, members, and political repute bore no proportion to the fuss and noise. The sections left the Route du Chêne at first for quarters in the Rue du Rhône, in a decrepit public-house; and afterwards for a back room in the brasserie of the Quatre Saisons, near the Grotto; but their funds were low and their enrolments few. The Radicals of Geneva were against them; and the followers of Fazy broke into their meeting, and disturbed them by an adverse vote.

In brief, the great battalion would not march. The workmen could not pay their centimes, trust their brothers with the cash-box, shut their eyes in silence, and await the birth of a new world. The clatter in the papers served them well enough; but all that talk of millions would not pay their printer's bills. They must have more subscribers on their books, and they could only gain these paying members by adopting one of the great party cries. They must return in practice to the living politics of their age. It was a sad necessity in the eyes of Tolain, man of study; but he could not help the facts. While he was puzzling out his problems, duns were knocking at his door with unpaid bills.

One delegate from Belgium, six delegates from England, seventeen from France, six from Germany, two from Italy, and thirty-one from Switzerland, came together in a room of the Casino at Lausanne. Three only of the deputies from England were of English name. England was mainly represented by two German tailors and a French fiddle-maker. Germany was represented by two doctors, one professor, an hotel-keeper, a machinist, and a gentleman of no profession that he cared to name. Italy was represented by two doctors, Stamfa and Tomasi. Four professors, three journalists, and a commercial agent, represented the toilers of Zürich and Geneva. Observe that here is not a gathering of the craftsmen, bent on study of the questions which affect them in their hours of work and in their rate of pay, but an assembly of middle-class dreamers and theorists. Eugène Dupont, the French delegate from Greek Street, took the chair, and here began and ended England's interest in the congress. Carter, perfumer, Swan, ribbon weaver, and Walton, architect, the three delegates with English names, were silent; and for any active bearing on the congress, London might have been a million miles away.

So soon as it was found that if the young society was to live they must connect themselves with politics, division broke upon their ranks. The Switzer,

Russ, and Belgian were, in fact, more communistic and political than the French, and since M. Tolain had no longer a majority of votes, the conference took a communistic and political colour far too red for him. Cæsar de Paëpe, the Belgian delegate, proposed that congress should declare, in principle, that land in every country is the common property of all. If this great principle were adopted, he was ready to go on. He would propose, as a beginning, to abolish the right of inheritance in certain stages and degrees. It was the first attack on private property, and Tolain told the congress he would fight against it to his death.

But communistic views came out on many points. To wit, the following motions were adopted

"Congress earnestly invites the members of the International in all countries to use their utmost influence to induce the trades unions to employ their funds in founding co-operative mills and workshops.

"Congress admits that mutual help should be given in every attempt to raise the rate of wages, while declaring that a higher end is yet to be attained in the suppression of wages altogether.

"Congress decides that all religious teaching should be discarded from public education.

"Congress is of opinion that the judges should be chosen by universal suffrage.

"Congress affirms that the social emancipation of the working class is inseparable from their political emancipation, and that the establishment of political liberty is the first measure absolutely required."

Congress also expressed an opinion that "a universal language" and a "better system of spelling words" would be great advantages to the working men. The doctors did not say which language should prevail; but as the argument was French, it was understood in congress that the "universal language" must be French. With some improvement "in spelling words" it was supposed that English and American artisans would soon pick up the idiom of Voltaire.

Then came the fight on Cæsar de Paëpe's motion; for this motion is a gage of war between the Communists and Socialists; the enemies of private property in all its forms, and those who urge that private property is the basis of a perfect social state. The English, German, Swiss, and Belgians were, on the whole, in favour of the doctrine that the land belongs to all; that is to say, these communistic views were held by the two German tailors and the French fiddle maker who represented England, by De Paëpe, printer, who represented Belgium, by the six professors and mechanics who represented the Fatherland. The two Italians, and a majority of the seventeen Frenchmen, spoke and voted for the maintenance of private rights in land, as well as in the machinery by which that land is watered, drained, and ploughed. Many of the Swiss supported the French and Italian delegates; contending that the adoption of this Belgian motion would involve them in a fatal march towards Communism pure and simple, but the doctors were so numerous and so noisy that their utmost efforts only just sufficed to get the vote postponed until the coming year.

In a final meeting a proposal was submitted and adopted for connecting the International with the republican movement of the time. Little could be done unless the active democrats would join their ranks; and Tolain, much against his judgment, was compelled by pressure of opinion in the congress "to give hostages" to the unborn republic. "It was a false move," says Fribourg dolefully, "but one that should have given us some results." It was not long in giving them results in lodging most of them in jail!

CHAPTER XVII

A New Alliance

W hile these professors, doctors, and commercial agents were amazing Canton Vaud with edicts on co-operation, strikes, exchanges, and the right of property in land, another body of fanatics were distracting Canton Geneva in the cause of liberty and peace. Gustave Chaudey (afterwards murdered by the Communards), was one of those who raved about perpetual peace and universal love. No party in Geneva liked these visitors, who talked of peace, while representing the extremest party of the barricades. One M. Barny, driven from Paris into exile, had set up this League of Peace and Liberty, which must not be confounded with the Society of Peace. M. Rollanday, a Swiss engraver, joined M. Barny, bringing into the new society Michael Bakounin, the Russian communist-colleague of Herzen and friend of Marx.

Bakounin is a Moscovite of Tartar name and blood. In early life he was involved in some mysterious plot, condemned to the Siberian mines, and carried in a tarantass across the Oural chain. Herzen and Ogareff[1] were his companions in offence, and, like him, they were sentenced to the mines. All three escaped; no one knew how. Of Herzen some account was given in a mendacious book, which bore his name, but parts of which he afterwards disclaimed. Bakounine was in prison at the mines. One day it was announced in Paris that Bakounine was in Europe. How he managed to escape the mines is still a secret. By what route he left Siberia is not known. Some say he came to Europe from the West. He certainly has been in the United States, of which he is a "citizen," by customary entry at New York. The Moscovite conspirators came to Geneva as a pleasant place, not far from Paris and from Genoa, the two volcanic centres of their faith. They found no rest, but wandered to and fro about the earth. A cloud

---

1   Nikolay Ogarev (1813–1877) was born into a liberal-minded aristocratic family. He and Alexander Herzen had been childhood friends and both studied at Moscow University, where they became involved with utopian socialist circles. —Ed.

Mikhail Bakunin

attracted them; a storm compelled them. Herzen went to Paris and to London, where he edited his *Kolokol*. Ogareff joined him in St. John's Wood. Bakounine settled in Geneva. They were known as men who go beyond republicans and Socialists. Bakounine is an open Nihilist; a man who makes a creed of pure negation, denying everything—religion, virtue, history, man and God. In one of the many Saxon risings, he obtained in mockery the name of Roi de Saxe; but he delights to call himself a Russian Savage, in contempt for our society, our learning, and our civilization. He avows himself an atheist. He is an enemy of private property in land. He is said to hold the marriage bond in high contempt. He hates all forms of law, repudiates all claims of power.

This man of many callings—Russian Savage, Roi de Saxe, and Citizen of the United States—was Pontiff of the League of Peace and Liberty, then sitting in the Electoral Palace of Geneva. The Republic built this palace for the people; it is always granted on the application of a citizen; and congresses of many sorts are held within its walls. It would be lent to Spurgeon; it has been lent to Train. But these disciples of Bakounine, instead of busying themselves with peace and liberty, were yelling at the Pope of Rome, the Czar of Russia and the Queen of Spain, and passing resolutions calling on the members of the League to war with tyrants, till oppressors of the people have been cut off root and branch. The Genevese got vexed; men met and wrangled on the quays; and quarrels in the cafés led to angry threats. When the delegates from Lausanne came in with news that the International Association had recognised the League of Peace and Liberty, they found the Electoral Palace crowded with a mob of Swiss Radicals, followers of Fazy, who were voting every motion down, and threatening to toss these foreign orators into the Rhone.

Chaudey caught up this news from Lausanne, and, rushing to the tribune, moved the adoption of a solemn Pact, by which the working classes and the middle classes should be reconciled for ever—the working-classes helping the middle-classes to regain their lost political power, the middle-classes helping the working-classes to remove all obstacles to their economical redemption. Bursts of cheering greeted Chaudey; artisans and advocates embraced each other; and, with cries of "Long live the Universal Republic!" his proposal was adopted by the League.

The Fazyites were rather puzzled how to act; a mob of Radicals does not like to fight with Radicals; and as the deputation from the International Working Men's Association stood beside the Leaguers in that moment of enthusiasm, the local storm rolled by without much harm being done. But Chaudey's solemn Pact of Peace was utterly rejected by the revolutionary clubs of Paris; and his effort to combine the middle classes and the lower classes in a common cause was afterwards accepted by the Communards as a sufficient warrant for his death.

CHAPTER XVIII

The Paris Branch Dissolved

O n his return to Paris, Tolain found that this new Pact with the political men involved him and his friends in every movement and emotion of the day. They had to play their part in the funeral of Daniel Manin, the Venetian patriot; in the protests made against the Roman expedition; in the banquet given to Combatz, the wounded Garibaldian; in the conference with the deputies of Paris; in the series of events which followed in their train. All kinds of trouble grew upon them; with the deputies for Paris, who were members of the middle classes; with the captains of the revolution, who were jealous of their influence in the workshops; with the Government, which, now that they had come into the field of politics, began to watch them with a jealous eye. A great event was to be made of Daniel Manin's funeral, as a protest of the capital against the Roman expedition; and the revolutionary circles wrote to ask the deputies of Paris to attend the ceremony at Montmartre. As these deputies sent no answers, some of them being in the country, others not disposed to venture limb and life, the International Association called on Jules Favre, (who was known to be in Paris,) and his colleagues, to resign their seats in the Assembly, and thus to bring the Government face to face with the electors on the great affair of Rome.

Jules Favre, receiving a deputation of working men in his hotel, protested against the form, a little too imperious, of their message; but he told them he accepted, in principle, their policy of resignation, if the whole body of the deputies for Paris could be got to act in common. For a single deputy to resign was useless if not worse, for it would seem to censure, by a public act, the conduct of those colleagues who could not see things as the single deputy saw them. Would the other deputies resign? He thought they would refuse: and standing by himself, he could not yield his trust. They put a capital query, "If the working men allow the liberal middle class to guide them, will you be ready when the time to take up arms shall come?" At once the advocate replied, "You, gentlemen of the workshop, you, and you only, made the Empire; and it is for you who made it to unmake it. "These gentlemen of the workshop took a fierce dislike to the Republican deputy, whose splendid rooms and flashy logic were an insult to their pinching poverty and native sense. From this night there was feud between the International Association and the Parliamentary Republicans, which time has only served to turn into a war of life and death.

The banquet given to Combatz, who was shot down by a chassepot at Mentana, introduced Fribourg to Raoul Rigault, afterwards so notorious as a leader of the Commune. Rigault took the founder of the International aside, and told him that he-Raoul Rigault—was the happy author of a device for silencing reactionists, without the spilling of one drop of blood. For Rigault was a tender-hearted man, who could not bear the sight of blood. To spare the nerves of timid people, he had made a wonderful machine. His plan, he said, might be divided into two main parts; in only one of which a little blood might have to flow. For when the hour to rise should come, a band of stout young fellows would be sent to the houses of such persons as it was well to kill at once, and having got inside their rooms, these stout young men should either brain or shoot them on the spot. A list of names and domiciles was prepared and marked. Each youth would have his weapon and his list. The work of death would be achieved in every part of Paris in a single night. This scene would usher in the play in

Raoul Rigault

which he was to prove his science. All the ministers and officers of the Empire, all the canting deputies of the Left, and all the sparks and fribbles of the upper class would be arrested in their beds, conducted to a caserne, driven into a court, and when they had been jammed and pressed together, he would play upon them shocks and flashes from an electrical battery of enormous power.

"Is not my battery a brave machine?" cried Rigault, with a laugh; "there will not be a drop of blood!"

At length M. Rouher was prepared to strike his blow.

One night a body of police broke into the Rue des Gravilliers, seized such books and papers as they found, and afterwards moved on the lodgings of Tolain, Chemalé, Heligon, Murat, and eleven others, whom they carried off to jail. At first M. Rouher thought he could indict these fifteen prisoners for conspiracy; but any such intention had to be abandoned for the want of proof. He then fell back upon the charge of belonging to a secret society; but, here again the lawyers led him into error; for on careful study of the documents, he saw that such a charge might fail. How could he satisfy a jury that the International was a secret body? All their congresses were open; all their plans were published. Any one could find the Paris Branch at No. 44, Rue des Gravilliers. Rouher felt that such a charge must fail him, and he gave instructions that his prisoners should be tried as members of a society not authorised by law.

It is possible that Napoleon was dreaming still of an alliance with these serious artisans, who were, in truth, the only men in Paris whom a Throne, supported by an army like the French, had cause to fear. The judge, M. Delesvaux, and the Imperial prosecutor, treated them with kindness and respect. "The prisoners who appear before you," said the Imperial prosecutor to the Court, "are industrious, honest, and intelligent working men. They have never been condemned before to-day. No stain is on their moral character. In justifying the course we take against them, I have not one word to say that will attaint their honour." Tolain conducted the defence, which occupied two sittings of the Court. Of course they were condemned. M. Delesvaux gave his judgment:

"The International Working Men's Association, established in Paris under the designation of Bureau of Paris, is dissolved.

"Each prisoner is condemned to pay a fine of 100 francs."

Tolain appealed against this verdict, but the sentence was confirmed. The Imperial Government was supported by the Imperial courts of law. The Bureau of Paris was dissolved, and the International Working Men's Association ceased to have a legal existence on the soil of France.

CHAPTER XIX

Ste. Pelagie

onsieur Rouher, having struck his blow, was tempted by his cheap success, to try again. Some men were still at large towards whom he bore an ancient grudge, for instance, Bourdon, who had foiled him in his pet imperial scheme. He sent his agents to arrest nine others—Bourdon, Varlin, Combault, Mollin, Humbert, Landrin, Granjon, Malon, and Charbonneau, whom he swept into the prison of Ste. Pelagie.

Among the crowds of prisoners there detained for trial, was Cluseret, who called himself General Cluseret, and claimed to be a "citizen" of the United States. This man soon made himself the evil genius of their cause.

Cluseret had been a captain in the French army; he had served with credit in Algiers and Russia; but some question had arisen about the regimental funds; and Cluseret, who had kept the books and moneys, was compelled to quit the ranks. He served with Garibaldi in the Two Sicilies; he served with Fremont in the United States. He quarrelled with his leaders, and he left them—not without his meed of honour. As a mark of his sincere appreciation, he bestowed upon himself the rank of general.

As General Cluseret he returned to Europe, with the mission of reporting to the Fenian Circles of New York on English arsenals, magazines, and ports of entry. Fenians recognised his rank of general; in return he recognised the Fenian Republic. Cluseret spent some time in London, studying how it might be captured, held, and burnt. He went to Woolwich, where he was received by Fenian circles as their military chief. He went about the dockyards and the workshops unobserved at least, he thought so; and he studied on the spot the means of a surprise that would astound the world, and paralyse at once the English army and the English fleet. How little came of all these studies, every reader is aware. The Fenian general saw no opening for a fight. He went to Ireland, to denounce the Irish people as a pack of whelps; and when he found himself in trouble he appealed to the Republic for protection, and our Government

allowed him to escape. He crossed the Straits to
France, where he engaged in plots to overthrow
the Government in favour of the Duc d'Aumale;
but as the Duc d'Aumale was wise enough to hold
his tongue and close his purse, the self-appointed
Fenian general passed once more into the Democratic camp. A few months led him to Ste. Pelagie,
where he again invoked the Stars and Stripes.

A man of dark designs and dubious fame, who
cared for neither Empire nor Republic, but who
longed to rule and reign, no matter in what camp,
the Fenian general made advances to the artisans whom Rouher's policy had sent into his pris-
on-yard. He saw in these poor toilers dupes and
tools whose anger he could turn to good account.
Their offices were closed, their papers seized, their
persons outraged by the Government, and as they
spoke like earnest men, he thought they might be
worked upon to join the revolutionary armies—
they and all their fellows of the late society to take
up arms and chase away the despots who had done
them all these wrongs. He lured them into chat, he
entered into all their views, he suffered in their trials, and he proffered them his aid. The men were
taken by his talk, and some of them inclined to see
in him their friend and leader. Bourdon held aloof;
but Varlin, Malon, Humbert, and some others
listened to the tempter's voice. For Cluseret was
quick, adroit, and able; he had seen the world; he
had a footing in the Great Republic; and he knew
the use of arms, the discipline of camps, and the

impediments and resources of a civil war. Annoyed by the suppression of their bureau, and their personal arrest, the men were in a fitting mood for listening to a voice like that of Cluseret. The General told them everything depended on themselves. The world was theirs, and they might have it when they pleased. But they could only take their own when they had learnt to use their strength. They were a mob, they must become an army. "You are masters," he exclaimed in confidence to Varlin, Malon, and the rest, "but you can only exercise your power on one condition—you must organise—organise—organise! Demand success from organisation, and success will never be refused."

Two months after the condemnation of Tolain and the first group of members, Varlin and the second group of members were brought up. M. Delesvaux presided as before. Varlin, acting as counsel for the whole, confessed in loud and pointed words that he and his companions were republicans and communists. They were condemned to fines; the Paris Bureau was again declared dissolved.

CHAPTER XX

A Bonapartist Move

nd now began the secret efforts of the working men, in company with the friends whom some of them had found in prison yards, to fight the Government underground. They tried to keep their bureau, but in vain: for scarcely any of their members dared to leave their names on books which might be seized. They had to give up bureau, sections, officers, and organisation, and to form a secret band of brethren, who engaged to pay their fees, to propagate their principles, and act on orders from a central point. They sought in this new field of action for some means of bringing all the trade societies of Paris which were either authorised or tolerated under one control, by founding a federal chamber, in which these trades might all be present in the person of their delegates. Their efforts met with some success, and for a time the work proposed by the original founders of the International seemed likely to be done. The new body, called the Federals, met in council, levied funds, supported strikes, and took the side of labour in all trade disputes.

M. Rouher took alarm once more, for neither lawyer nor police could say in what these Federals differed as to public action from the Internationals.

The same men—the same rules—the same ends—the same means, were in the first society and in the last. Unless these institutions could be turned into supports of the Imperial system, they were too important to be left alone. Could anything be done to bring these people, who might be so hostile in a plebiscite, so dangerous in an insurrection, into friendly attitude towards Cæsar? "Yes," replied a voice to which the Bonapartes had sometimes listened in their secret councils, "something may be done" The voice was that of Armand Levi, one of those democrats who supped at the Palais Royal and maintained relations, more or less uneasily, with the Republican refugees in London, Brussels, and Geneva.

A Jew of French descent, this Armand Levi had attached himself to the Napoleons at an early time, and was employed by them in various ways. He

Armand Lévy

acted as a secretary to Adam Mickievicz, the Polish poet, who lived in France, and called the first Napoleon the Messiah of the modern world. Levi helped to edit his remains a useful service to the Second Empire. Afterwards he came to Geneva, where he edited a Democratic paper in a strong Napoleonic sense. His efforts were not fruitless even in Geneva, and a party was created to applaud the modern Cæsar and support his throne. In other countries, too—in England, Italy, the United States a fashion of admiring Cæsar and his works began to spread. A clever, plausible, and learned man, this Levi thought he might be useful in the Belgian capital while the congress would be there, and so the secret agent was allowed to go and see what could be done. The Federals were the International under another name. Rouher had warned these Federals; but no action had as yet been taken for suppressing them; and he was free as yet to take his final course. He might permit the Federals to exist within the law; the Federals might enter the International as a branch. In fact, if Levi found the parties willing to agree, it would be easy to arrange the terms. To Brussels Armand Levi went.

The Paris Bureau having been dissolved, no delegate from Paris could appear in Brussels. Tolain was afraid that in the necessary absence of the men from Paris, and in the necessary silence of the men from London, the disciples of Universal Communism would prevail in speech and vote. To meet an evil, which was nothing less than ruinous to his cause, he begged the General Council sitting in Soho to change the form of invitation, so that persons could attend the congress who either represented a trade society or were members of a Socialist club. It was against his former policy, but he was forced by the Imperial courts to either let these unknown men come in or leave his empty benches to the German and the Russ. He chose what seemed to him a lesser evil; but he knew it was an evil: and he took the train to Belgium with a heavy heart.

When he arrived in Brussels he was staggered by the aspect of affairs. Instead of finding working men and students, he encountered in the streets and galleries of that town a crowd of doubtful persons. There was Henri Rochefort, swinging his feverish Lanterne to and fro; there was Armand Levi, with a Bonapartist programme in his pocket; there was Godin-Lemaire, founder of the Familistère; there was Blanqui, master of the barricades; there was Becker, German Communist from Geneva; there was Dupont, the fiddle-maker, who had ceased to represent London in favour of Naples; there were crowds of others equally unwelcome in his sight. His fears were quickly justified by facts.

About a hundred delegates, with many persons who were not delegates, met in the ante-room of the Brussels Circus. London was represented by three Englishmen, two German tailors, one Swiss watchmaker, one French mechanic, and a Jew tobacconist. France was weak; and Italy had no other delegate than the French fiddle maker, Dupont.

Johann Philipp Becker

The Communists, as Tolain feared, were in a vast majority, and when Hermann Jung—a master of the lingoes—took the chair, these Communists insisted on proceeding to a vote on what they held to be the capital question—that of a common property in the soil. "They would have no rule and order," says Fribourg; "neither that of property nor that of liberty." They voted in an overwhelming phalanx for the following propositions

Land is common property, and cannot be owned by private persons.

Woods and forests are common property.

Mines and coal pits are common property.

Roads, canals, railways, and telegraphs are common property.

Agricultural machines are common property.

A general proposition was then moved and carried, that in principle every sort of property belongs to all citizens in common.

Tolain wished to speak against these motions, but the audience hissed and hooted him—the actual father of the International, and the only man in that assembly who had suffered in the cause! Poor Tolain stood alone, as founder. Fribourg was in Bern, attending to the League of Peace and Liberty, in which his principles were threatened by the speculative communism of Bakounine. Varlin was in Paris, shut up in Ste. Pelagie, where his principles were threatened by the practical communism of Cluseret. But Tolain, though he stood alone, would not be silent.

He demanded to be heard. He raised his voice in the name of Liberal France. A storm of opposition to him rose. Dupont, who was presiding at the moment, gave him no support. Instead of urging that the delegate from Paris must be heard, he put it to the meeting, whether Paris, in the person of M. Tolain, should be heard or not. A vast majority was against him, and he sat down in despair. The Liberal cause was lost.

CHAPTER XXI

The Swiss Alliance

wo currents of opinion were observed among the delegates in the ante-rooms of the Brussels Circus; one current leading them towards Socialism with a Cæsar in the front; a second current leading them towards Universal Communism of the Anabaptist type. They had their choice of these two forms—which would they take an Emperor Napoleon or a John of Leyden?

One of these two forms was advocated by Armand Levi; the other by Philip Becker. Armand Levi represented the possibilities of an Imperial

Socialism; Philip Becker represented the prospects of a Universal Communism.

By birth Bavarian, by adoption Swiss, by predilection French, by trade a brushmaker, by choice an agitator, by necessity a soldier, Philip Becker, once of Frankenthal, now of Geneva, had served and suffered in his cause. A brave captain, an able writer, he had never changed his side, had never faltered in his faith, although his chief rewards for forty years of service had been prisons, poverty, and exile from his native land. All men respected him. Of late years he had given his energies to business, had improved his fortunes, and been able to assist his brethren in distress. He held on strictly to the communistic theories which he shared with Michael Bakounine, his friend and fellow-exile. In religion Becker and Bakounine were of one mind also; for they preached in many forms and phrases that religious feeling is a morbid growth, the Church a pestilential lazaretto, and the priesthood of all creeds and nations an incarnate fraud. There was no hope for man, they said, till he abolished God! Becker wished the International, now become thoroughly communistic, to absorb the League of Peace and Liberty, adopting all its programme and admitting all its members, male and female.

The terms suggested on behalf of Cæsar came too late. Ere Armand Levi spoke his cause was lost. Napoleon was no longer Cæsar. In the minds of these enthusiasts his star had fallen and his power had ceased. "You must understand," wrote Varlin, "that the Empire no longer exists, except in name."

The current of opinion represented by Becker— that of Universal and Collective Communism—had the greater strength, and Armand Levi left the circus in dismay. For some time he was lost to sight; yet he was toiling for his master in the dark; and when the barricades were built his name was in the Commune, and his voice was raised for the extremest counsels. He it was who rose in the Hôtel de Ville, to ask that all the deputies of Paris should be summoned from Versailles, and if they would not come, should be deposed, convicted, and condemned to death!

After five or six fancy resolutions had been voted in the Brussels circus, Albert Richard, typographer, of Lyons, was deputed to attend the League of Peace and Liberty in Bern, and tell the members of that wild society that the International Association had adopted them.

Albert Richard, a Communist of extremest views, repaired from Brussels to Bern, where Michael Bakounine, the Russian Savage, was amazing every one by his great scheme for equalising functions and capacities in all our classes, and in both our sexes. Of a giant's height, and yet with patient eyes, the Russian rose, and in a voice like bursting winds, he claimed from the assembly an expression of the conscience, brief and prompt. Would they concede equality of sex as well as class? Without this vote there was no justice, there could be no peace. Down with this civilisation founded on slavery! "I am not a Communist, but a Collectevist," he roared; " I demand the abolition of inheritance." Richard supported him, in the name of the International. "The cure," said Richard, "is a common property of the soil. We must impose a democratic tax." Jaclard lifted up his voice; he was a Collectevist, not a Mutualist; he was an Atheist, and out of Atheism there was no hope for man."To be religious is to be ridiculous; if you are not Atheists, you are the property of despots; and in place of being a league of helots you will be a Holy Alliance against the Revolution "Fribourg, Chaudey, and Lemonnier combated these views in the name of liberal Paris and of liberal France. For these are not so much the views of working men, as of professors and philosophers. Richard took the other side, supporting Bakounine's proposal for equality of class and sex, not only for himself, but for the trade associations in whose name he spoke. Bakounine, beaten on the test by 80 votes to 30, left the hall-he and his faithful flock of sheep—in dudgeon, casting off the dust from his feet against his colleagues. Next day, the thirty Irreligious Communists sent in their resignations to the League, and started a new society—The International Alliance of the Socialist Democracy, as a branch of the International Working Men's Association.

Geneva was declared to be head-quarters of the new Alliance; Geneva being the residence of Becker, its soldier, and Bakounine,its high priest.

This new society had the frankness to announce itself at once. "The Alliance declares itself Atheist," were the first words of its appeal. "It seeks the abolition of all creeds; the substitution of science for faith, and of human justice for divine." "It seeks before all things to equalise classes and individuals of both sexes." "It declares that all property should be held in common, and all children should be fed, clothed, and taught in the same manner." "It supports the cause of labour against capital." "It repudiates all idea of patriotism and nationality in favour of the Universal Democracy."

The first to sign these articles of faith was Philip Becker, the second Michael Bakounine. Eighty-three others followed, six of whom were women.

In an evil hour the London council—few of whom could know what they were doing—suffered this Swiss Alliance to become a branch of the International Association. The English members, from their want of languages, were at the mercy of the French and German members, and especially of the learned few. Marx overruled them by his strength of will, although he kept his name concealed from public gaze. Through Marx, and his convenient tool Eccarius, the Greek Street conclave were misled. Bakounine and his party of avowed Communists and Atheists were admitted; and the International Association—though the English members could not see it—had an uncrowned pontiff and an uncrowned prince; a pontiff in the Russian Savage, and a ruler in the German Jew.

Pierre Vésinier

CHAPTER XXII

Down! Down!

rom Bern to London—from the open congress to the public-house. Six weeks after the new Alliance had been formed in Switzerland, M. Vésinier, secretary of the French section of the International in London, called a meeting of that section to denounce the men of moderate councils, to declare the International a political body, to announce, in spite of Tolain and Lucraft, Fribourg and Odger, that the Association of Workmen was a Republican society, reddest of the red, and blackest of the black.

Vésinier, a man of some small talent in the writing line, with heated veins, a narrow understanding, and a flighty head, had been a member from an early date, though not a leader in the movement. From the first he had mistaken Tolain's purpose, and in writing for the press had put their doings in a broader light than they were meant to bear. Tolain wrote to him. He answered with disdain. An author of repute—of ill-repute, the chasers and engravers of the Rue des Gravilliers said—Vésinier would not have his articles controlled by working men. He was supposed to be the author of some personal and political squibs much talked about just then. So great a man could not permit his leaders to be handled by such fellows. But the workmen paid him back in his own coin; bad blood was made between them; and the angry author challenged four of his critics to a bout of swords and pistols. They accepted his proposals; for in such affairs as duels the Paris working men have no more sense than journalists and soldiers; but the congress of Geneva coming on, both sides consented to postpone the combat until after the festival of fraternity in the Route du Chêne. While the thing was pending, Vésinier was imprisoned by the Government for an attack upon the Empress in his *Marriage of a Spanish Lady* which was lucky for him, Fribourg says, as otherwise "the Paris correspondents of the International would have killed him like a dog." Some other works have made this man a name. *The New Cæsar* and *Nights at St. Cloud* have been a good deal read—far more, indeed, than they deserve.

Vésinier, being in London, called a meeting of French refugees in a public-house, where he denounced certain members of the International—such as Odger and Potter—who would not allow him to make the society political, and where, in the names of Paris and of France, he made a proclamation that the International Association was republican, democratic, socialistic, and universal; a society having the same principles, the same ends, and the same means as the revolutionary Commune of Paris. In the eyes of Vésinier, as in those of Varlin, the preliminary task of the International was over; all that study could achieve for them was done; and now their duty was to change the International into the Commune.

Even after it was seen that Armand Levi had not been able to allure the workmen towards the Bonapartes, the Government were slow to strike the Federals in Paris. Nearly all these syndicates and circles had been authorised. The Government had been trying through these trade societies to turn the thoughts of working men to social questions; and to smite these circles was to enter on a war with men whose answer to an edict might be barricades. To interrupt their meetings would appear a stretch of power, and day by day the Government was finding people less and less disposed to hear of arbitrary acts. No doubt the courts of law would do M. Rouher's bidding; he had but to ring his bell and in an hour the Federals might be in the yards of Ste. Pelagie; but he was wise enough to see that such high measures had become too perilous for him to take. His master was not what he had been. It was better, he conceived, to stay his hand until the public, taught by what was passing and preparing round them, would support him in a more decided course.

A congress was about to meet in Basel, where the question would be put and voted, whether the trade societies in Paris and elsewhere should not be turned into revolutionary committees—not to study the Utopia and the Age of Reason, but the art of confiscating property and over-setting thrones. Napoleon knew Bakounine, and might shrewdly guess that since the International Association had adopted the Swiss Alliance, the Swiss Alliance would adopt the International, extinguish it, and take its place. If that should come to pass, the Working Men's Association would be publicly announced as Atheistic and Communistic. From that day the Emperor might fairly count on finding France and even Paris on his side, in any measures of repression he might think it wise to take. His present wisdom seemed to stand apart and watch.

CHAPTER XXIII

Congress of Basel

T he fourth and final congress of the International Working Men's Association met in Basel. England was represented as before by three English—mostly silent members—by two Germans, and by one Switzer. Robert Applegarth, carpenter, Benjamin Lucraft, cabinet-maker, and Cowel Stepney, editor of the *Social Economist*, were the three English on the roll. Friedrich Lessner and George Eccarius were the German tailors who had so often done us the honour to bear our flag in public. Hermann Jung, watch-maker, of Clerkenwell, was the Switzer who assisted them to hold that flag aloft. The French were weak in talent and divided in opinion. Fribourg was not with them; Varlin had gone over to the Communists; and Tolain was depressed in soul and spirit. A presentiment that the International was about to perish seized upon his heart and almost paralysed his voice. No common field of action could be found, for nearly every delegate had come to represent a different school. Chemalé was a Mutualist; Tartaret was a Liberalist; Varlin was a Communist; Mollin was a Positivist; Langlois was a Collectivist. Spain was represented by a printer and a physician. The United States sent out a journalist, who could represent and ply his trade. The journalists were many. Bohemia sent a journalist in Neumayer, editor of the *Neustädter Wochenblatt*; Austria sent a journalist in Oberwinder; Saxony sent a journalist in Krieger. Germany had, of course, a legion of her pundits present. Liebknecht, member of the Prussian Parliament and editor of the *Wochenblatt* was there; Professor Janach of Magdeburg was there; Rittinghausen of Cologne, was there; Becker, of Frankenthal, was there. Belgium had nearly as many professors from her universities as craftsmen from her factories. Professor Robin, of Liege, and Professor Hins, of Brussels, took their seats. M. Brismée, a Communistic printer, also took his seat. Geneva sent Armand Goegg, editor of *Das Felleisen*, one of those foreign theorists who had made her soil their home. Neufchatel was represented by Professor Gillaume, Chaux-de-Fonds by

Professor Robert. Basel named Herr Bruhin, publicist, to give her vote.

At Basel, Michael Bakounine, man of many names and countries; Roi de Saxe—American citizen and Russian Savage—made his first appearance in a congress of the International—his first appearance and his last; for after he had once appeared all further talk was useless. Let him speak the word and everything that could be said was said. A Nihilist, his mission was to clear the ground in front, not only of such filth as emperors, popes, and kings, but such absurdities as congresses and presidents. When Basel heard the voice of wisdom she might rest in peace for Bakounine came in all the splendour evermore of his representative dignity—the universal man. He represented Russia by his birth, America by his letters of naturalisation, Saxony by his title, Canton Geneva by his residence, Canton Basel by his presence, France and Italy by his delegated powers. He claimed to sit in congress as a delegate from the weavers of Lyons, and from the lazzaroni of Naples.

Karl Marx remained behind his cloud, content to rule the rulers and to keep the halo of his glory out of sight.

Hermann Jung

Chapter XXIV

A New International

Again the use of tongues determined the selection of a president. Three languages were necessary, and again the man who had the use of English, French, and German, was a foreign workman who had found a home in London. Hermann Jung, watchmaker, Clerkenwell, was chosen president; Brismée, of Brussels, and Bruhin, of Basel, were chosen vice-presidents. These men were Communists of the deepest shade.

The Communistic party was much stronger in the Congress of Basel than it had been in the Congress of Brussels, and, in spite of gallant efforts on the part of Tolain and his friends, the principle of confiscation was adopted. Varlin, Aubry, and some others of their colleagues, who had learned from Cluseret a higher doctrine than the International had taught them, quitted their ancient comrade on this vote. Bakounine asked for brief and nett resolutions.

"Inheritance is abolished."

"Ground-rent is abolished."

"The land belongs to the State."

"Society must be wound up."

This last demand of the Tartar pontiff, *la liquidation sociale*, not being clear to every one, Bakounine told the congress what he meant by winding up society. "I mean by winding-up society," he said, "the taking back, of right, all actual properties, by abolishing the political and judicial system which is the only sanction and safeguard of the present proprietors, and everything that calls itself legal right. I mean the taking back, in fact, of all and everything that one can seize, and just as fast as one can seize it, as events shall open out away." They knew it now, these doctors and philosophers; the Roi de Saxe laid bare the secrets of his heart. Old members of the International Association sat aghast. Even Paëpe could not go these lengths. In timid voice he argued that, with some exceptions for the public good, a father might be suffered to bequeath his savings to his child. But no, the Tartar would not hear of such abandonment of principle. "All productive work," he cried, "is necessarily collective work; even the work improperly called individual is the collective work of past generations. No inheritance, no personal property, no individualism!" Bakounine pressed his point. "I am an enemy," he roared above the heads of his astonished flock "I am a resolute enemy of the State and of the middle-class politics of the State. I demand the destruction of all societies, both national and territorial. I demand that on the ruins of these states we lay the foundations of a new society of working men."

A loud and frantic burst of welcome met these words. The Paris deputies, with few exceptions, fought against Bakounine, first and last, but a majority of doctors and professors were on his side. "Your proposals," said the Paris chasers and casters, are against logic, nature, history, and science." "Science!" shouted Brismée, the Brussels printer, "if science is against our revolutionary hopes, so much the worse for science. She must give way before our principles our principles shall give way to nothing." Roars of approbation greeted Brismée. Prof. Hins, Prof. Robin, Editor Goegg, and Pontiff Bakounine spoke in favour of abolishing private property; Tolain, Chemalé, Murat, and Mollin spoke against it. When the votes were counted, fifty-four were for it; only four against it. Private property was abolished.

Then a comic scene occurred. Having gained his point, Bakounine caused M. Brismée to bring up the next report from the committee recommending a complete and radical abolition of inheritance. It was a form, and nothing but a form. "Considering that Congress has declared that every sort of property is held in common, it is logically necessary to declare against inheritance," said Brismée, and the man was right. The Paris deputies were silent; they had made their protests on the capital clause; and here was but a detail of that clause. But when the votes were counted, thirty-two delegates were found to have voted with Bakounine, twenty-three against him. Seventeen members had declined to vote. His minor proposition was refused.

One of the two German tailors who were kind enough to represent English thought, Eccarius, took a middle course. When congress would not vote the extinction of inheritance, Eccarius proposed to tax succession for the public good by an ascending scale. This proposition was rejected also. Congress seemed afraid to think what it had done, in voting down private property, and could not be induced to back that vote by any subsequent proposal for carrying the principle into effect. Bakounine stormed, but storming at the delegates would not bring him votes. Varlin and Richard voted with him; and he was not wrong in thinking that these violent partisans would count for more in Paris and Lyons than more timid men. They carried the red flag aloft. Bakounine utterly despised that flag, as representing weak and partial counsels; but he knew the influence of that flag in France. He had to use the Paris delegates in his attempt to set aside the visible chieftainship of Odger, who was still the President in name.

Through the mouth of Louis Jean Pindy, carpenter, of Paris, he proposed an organisation, which was in fact a new society—a revolutionary society—a new International—to be formed out of the various syndicates, circles, clubs, and unions then existing—to be called a Federation of Trades—which was to have for aim and end resistance to all constituted powers. The English delegates supposed he meant resistance to the masters—aid, in fact, to strikes; but such was not Bakounine's limit. He is not a man to care for strikes, except so far as they are agencies of disorder and destruction. Pindy told his hearers how the sections of his new society would act. "The groups of these societies of resistance will form the future Commune, and the existing governments will be replaced by the councils of the trades unions." Pindy's propositions were adopted. From that hour the Working Men's International ceased to be; the name alone remained; but what was once a school of artisan philosophy was now a revolutionary body, bent on overturning churches, governments, societies, and laws.

To make the chaos more complete, Bakounine asked the congress to abolish the office of president. He moved this point in person. "Considering that it is unworthy of a society of working men to uphold a principle of monarchy and authority by allowing presidents, even though they exercise no actual power, and that honorary distinctions are an impeachment of democratic principles, congress engages all the sections, and all the working-men societies connected with the International, to abolish the office of presidency." This motion also passed, and Odger was put down.

With Odger fell the founders of the International; Tolain, Fribourg, all the men of peace and study. Tolain retired as Fribourg had retired. "The International of the French founders," says M. Fribourg, "was dead-quite dead"

The old society of thoughtful working men was gone; a new society of doctors, journalists, and professors had usurped its name and place. New men, new methods, and new purposes amazed the world. The men of study yielded to the men of strife. As Tolain fell, Bakounine rose; as Odger passed into the shadow, Marx came out into the light. Some English names were kept upon the roll, as blinds; but power was not now with them, even in that small degree to which they had been used. The people and the purposes were changed. Co-operatives sank into Communists; sections of study into circles of resistance. Members of the League of Peace and Liberty, whose emblem was the olive branch, whose motto was goodwill to men, were pledged to overturn the whole existing rule and order of the world!

Chapter XXV

The Temple

With a change of actors came a change of scene. If born in Paris and put to nurse in London, the "brat" had come out in Geneva. Geneva gave to it a motto and a flag, a priest, a soldier, and a creed. She wished to offer it a home. The votes in Basel having changed the International into an Alliance, Atheistic and Communistic, it was only fair that the direction of events should lie with those who had proposed this change of front. In London there was hardly any sympathy for the ideas introduced by Becker and Bakounine. Odger would not sign himself an atheist. Lucraft would not hear of barricades. Applegarth believed in private property. The foreign tailors might be drawn into the Communistic movement, but the English members lay beyond appeal. Till the society could march on Paris, and assume command in the Hôtel de Ville, Geneva, as the residence not only of Becker and Bakounine, but of Grosselin, Goegg, and Perret, was her natural home.

A temple worthy of their cult was sought and found. As yet the lodgings of the sections had been always cheap, obscure, and mean estaminets and brasseries in the poorer quarters of the town. Their last home was a beer-house called the Quatre Saisons, in the suburb of St. Gervais. No one cared to learn what they were doing in these dens. Park Lane is not disturbed by what is said in Kirby Street, nor is the Rue des Granges distressed by what a group of cobblers mutter in the Route du Chêne. But now a great and sudden change was made, and henceforth every public act was to be done beneath the porches and vineries of the richest people in the town.

Below the gardens of the Rue des Granges, on ground once covered by the guns of Fort de l'Oie, a group of new and handsome buildings has been raised—an Electoral Palace, a synagogue, a Conservatory of Music, a Masonic Temple, an Academy of Arts. Of these fine buildings, the Masonic temple—Temple Unique—is the first to catch a stranger's eye. This model of an old Greek edifice they hired. They put the name of Temple on their cards and bills. Their cult had gained a worthy shrine. In London worshippers might hold their service in the back room of a wretched shop; in Paris they might meet for study round a workman's bench; but in Geneva, near the dwelling of their pontiff, they were lodged in a grand edifice, with a semi-sacred and mysterious name.

How they had raised the funds, where they had got the introductions, were not known to citizens on the Quai des Bergues. A dozen stories flew about, and at the supper-tables of the Cercle des Mignons, where the best blood in Geneva is supposed to cool itself with iced champagne, you heard a sound of *Plonplon, always Plonplon*, whispered with a smile and shrug. Inquiry brought to light a curious fact. Prince Napoleon, in his several speculations, near and far, had lent a good round sum of money on the Temple and obtained possession of the title-deeds as mortgagee. Some weeks before the International got a footing in the Temple, Prince Napoleon sold his interest in the building to a speculator in such things. M. Baumgartner, the new owner, was a man of doubtful nationality. He was of German blood. He was a citizen of Geneva. He declared himself an English subject, and he travelled with an English passport. He had no objection, in the way of business, to be French. In fact, he was a citizen of the world. From this convenient man of business, by a process which remains a secret, the society procured a settlement in the Temple Unique on the Boulevard de Plainpalais.

A note was now sent from Geneva to London, calling on the General Council to disband. They had already put down Odger in obedience to the vote at Basel; but Bakounine and the revolutionary circles of Geneva felt that too much influence lay with No. 256, High Holborn, where the members, who had left their borrowed room in Greek Street, sat on cranky chairs and musty volumes. The supremacy of Paris-airy, bright, and passionate Paris-they could bear; but the supremacy of London—dull, prosaic, cautious London—they could never stand. The Council must dissolve. The time for barricades was near. The English were not men for such high courses; the initiative must always rest with France. What use was therein keeping up this form of governing from London? If the Council were dissolved, the English artisans would fall into their natural place in the association; as a province they would have their sections and their federations, managed by themselves, and dealing with their strikes, their nine-hours bills, and their co-operative stores. Their genius was too local for command; the revolutionary fire was wanting; and the communistic spirit had no hold upon them. Let them yield—Geneva said the foremost place.

CHAPTER XXVI

Proposed Revolution in England

ut such an abdication by the Council did not suit the policy of Marx. Marx lived in London; where he lived the International must have its seat. Of course, this personal reason was not urged. High ground of policy was taken for resisting such a change as that proposed from Switzerland. It may be doubted whether any English members of the International were aware of what was going on. The correspondence was in French—Eugène Dupont, the channel of communication; and the letters sent from London to Geneva were secret and confidential.

No more curious piece was ever written than the secret message posted by Dupont from London to Geneva on the 1st of January, 1870 (seven months before the war), explaining why the General Council of the International could not quit its English seat. Assuming, like his brethren of Geneva, that the time for a general rush to arms was near at hand, he laid down these five propositions

1. England is the only country in which a real Socialistic revolution can be made.

2. The English people cannot make this revolution.

3. Foreigners must make it for them.

4. The foreign members, therefore, must retain their seats at the London board.

5. The point to strike on first is Ireland, and in Ireland they are ready to begin their work.

The details of his message have an interest for the English reader, as exhibiting the views which foreigners, who live in London, studying how to light the flames of civil warfare, hold as to their chances of success. "England is the one country," writes Dupont, "in which the peasants have attained their utmost number, and the anded property has fallen into the fewest hands. It is the one country in which the capitalist, organising works upon the grandest scale, has thrown himself into every sort of production. It is the one country in which a vast majority consists of people paid by wages. It is the one country where the war of classes and the organisation of trade unions have acquired a certain degree of maturity and universality in consequence of their command of all the markets of the world." This last idea is of so much moment that the writer pauses in his tale to show the Beckers and Bakounines who are plotting in Geneva all its meaning. "If the landlords and the capitalists have their thrones in England, by a counter stroke of fortune the material means for their destruction are also found in England." What should be the consequences of such facts? A dissolution of the General Council? If that council were dissolved, the sections and the federations would be English, and the French and German refugees would lose their hold on the great societies. How would their prospects be improved by such a change? Dupont is frank enough to say, "The General Council having happily got its hand upon the great lever of the working-class revolution, what a folly—what a crime—it would be to allow this lever to pass into purely English hands!" That was an argument which Bakounine would under stand.

"These English," adds Dupont, "have all the materials needed for a Socialistic revolution; what they lack are the generalising spirit and the revolutionary fire." What then? Karl Marx, Eugène Dupont, and George Eccarius must clutch their power and keep their seats. They say so boldly. "It is only the General Council that can supply these prime defects that can accelerate the revolutionary movement in this country, and through this country in every other" They appeal in proof to what the journals of the dominant classes write of them—that is to say, that they have poisoned and extinguished the English spirit in our workshops, and prepared our artisans for a republican and communistic rising. "If you separate the General Council from the Provincial Council we shall lose the handling of the great lever. To give up our grave and secret labours (*l'action sérieuse et sousterraine*) would be a fault."

These gentlemen were aware that a revolutionary march is not an easy thing in London, where the people are so individual in their tastes and tempers, and so stupidly attached to independent judgment, private property, and personal rights. But they were not without some hope. In turning to the west they saw a star descending to the Irish Sea. That star they followed with beseeching eyes: it trembled over Cork. "The only point where we can strike the great blow against official England is on Irish soil. In Ireland the movement is made a hundred times more easy for us by the two prime facts that the social question is that of rent, and that the people are more revolutionary and exasperated than the English." All these reasons told against the change. A final phrase completed M. Dupont's account:

"The position of the International in face of the Irish question is very clear. Our first care is to push the revolution in England. To this end we must strike the first blow in Ireland "

Here is the situation on New Year's-day last year, six months after the disestablishment of the Irish Church!

Eugène Varlin

Chapter XXVII

Paris

onsieur Rouher, reading what had taken place at Basel, saw the time had come when he must either act against the Paris Federals, or drop at once the reins of power. These Federals, whom he had suffered to exist, were nothing less than the Societies of Resistance that were to form "the future Commune," while their syndicates and councils were those trade committees that were to replace existing governments when they fell. The Federation was the Commune—not yet housed in the Hôtel de Ville.

M. Rouher sent gendarmes into their unions to suppress them by superior orders in his master's name.

It was the last free sweep of Rouher's hand. Like Armand Levi's bid in Brussels, it was much too late. To be of use, it needed to be followed up by fresh arrests, fresh trials, and fresh judgments; but the Emperor shrank from such a course; and other causes helping to his ruin, Rouher fell, and weak Ollivier skipt upon his chair of thorns.

As the Napoleonic party failed in front, the Communistic party closed their ranks for an attack. Dupont wrote warmly from his office in High Holborn, urging Varlin, Malon, and the leaders who had driven out Tolain, Fribourg, and the students of economy from their own society, to organise the trades in Paris, in accordance with the law, if they could find away, but in defiance of the law, if such a way could not be found. The clever advocate whom they consulted could not find a way. At first they were compelled to seek, enrol, and organise their men in secret. All the trades of Paris were enflamed by the dispersion of their syndicates and clubs; in every auberge Varlin found recruits. As he declared, a few weeks later, it was as easy to enrol a fresh adherent as to drink a glass of beer. A month sufficed to make him bolder in his course. He now revived the Paris Bureau of the International in open and avowed defiance of the law.

Ollivier was too busy and too weak to trouble Varlin. In the great provincial towns this agent of the revolutionary Commune had his correspondents—one might almost say his ministers Richard in Lyons, Aubry in Rouen, Bastalica in Marseilles—

to whom he sent his orders with the utmost confidence that they would be observed. Pindy and
Johannard joined him in these efforts. They were
warned by Cluseret that if they meant to win they
must be organised. Pindy ran down to Brest, and
formed a section in that port. Johannard came to
Paris and established an influential section in the
Faubourg Saint Denis. The sections multiplied
themselves on every side, for now that the Association had a watchword and a flag—the barricade
and bonnet rouge—all revolutionary Paris rushed
into their ranks. They called themselves the Federals of the Paris branch of the International; they
were in fact the Commune marching stealthily on
the Hôtel de Ville.

What clouds were darkening over the Imperial house! The shot that murdered Victor Noir, the
publication of the *Marseillaise*, the arrest of Rochefort, the denunciations of Gustave Flourens,
and the trial of a Bonaparte for murder, came
upon each other quick and fast, too quick for any
government to stand, much less a government of
shift and trial, like the milk-and-water cabinet of
M. Ollivier. In the revolutionary clubs the Empire
was regarded as a corpse. Varlin sent out a circular in which he said, "What is of moment, first
and last, is to secure the triumph of the revolution.
Let us feel our strength. Let us draw our forces together. The cup is full. In a short time it will over-
flow. It is for the Revolution to choose its hour."
This circular was signed by Louis Eugène Varlin,

bookbinder, and Benoist Malon, shopman, both of whom were afterwards leading members of the Commune of Paris.

Varlin had selected Cluseret for his general, just as Cluseret had selected Varlin for his dupe. When Cluseret was liberated from Ste. Pelagie, mainly on the ground of his American citizenship, the Government requested him to quit a land in which he had no longer any civil rights. He sailed for New York, in which he strove to spread some knowledge of the new Federalist principles adopted by Varlin and his brother Communists. He never entered the society as a member, for he meant to be the master, not the equal, of these chasers, bookbinders, and shop men. Varlin sent him news from Paris, which he answered in more fervid phrase. The Federals of France were taught to look on Cluseret not only as their soldier when the hour of strife should sound, but as the general (vice Garibaldi, who, not being a Communist, could not be trusted) of the Red Republic of all Nations. He was French, and in the universal revolution now impending it was fit that France should hold the sword. He was a citizen of the United States, from which Republic it was fair to count on instant recognition and support. He was a Fenian general, and the first explosion of the social strife was then expected to take place on Irish soil. He had been much in England, studying dockyards, arsenals, and strategic points, and England was supposed to be the more immediate theatre of the Communistic war. All happy qualities and accidents appeared in Cluseret, and Varlin was instructed to recall him from New York.

Varlin offered him the chief direction of his army. Cluseret replied, "I need not tell you that I accept your offer, and shall give myself to the work of being useful to my brothers in toil and misery." Cluseret cared no more for strikes and hours of labour than Karl Marx, but he was ready to become their agent in New York until he could become their generalissimo in Paris. "I shall soon be with you," he continued, "but I have yet to organise the French and American groups. You say success is certain. So it is, if we prepare the ground beforehand. When the day arrives we shall be ready; physically as well as morally ready." Then he adds the sentence: "When that day shall come, it will be either Us or nothing! Paris will be Ours, or Paris will have ceased to be!"

This announcement from New York that Paris was to yield or perish, bears the date of February 17, 1870.

The sword of Cluseret was to flash more terribly in the eyes of all reactionists than the battery of Rigault. Perhaps no plan for burning Paris had been yet contrived; but Cluseret's letter leaves no doubt that months before the war with Prussia gave the Communists a chance of opening their campaign against society in France instead of Ireland, the man who called himself a Fenian General, and studied how to break and burn the English dockyards, had resolved that if he failed in his designs on Paris, Paris should be levelled with the ground.

The secret history of the International Association passes at this point into the secret history of the Revolutionary Commune. In another year, Varlin, Pindy, Malon, Johannard, Vésinier, and Cluseret, were all at the Hôtel de Ville.

FINIS

Index

www.ingramcontent.com/pod-product-compliance
Lightning Source LLC
Chambersburg PA
CBHW030943150426
42812CB00071B/3380/J